BARRY BONDS

TITLES IN THE SERIES
BASEBALL'S ALL-TIME GREATEST HITTERS

Hank Aaron

Barry Bonds

Ty Cobb

Joe DiMaggio

Lou Gehrig

Rogers Hornsby

Joe Jackson

Willie Mays

Stan Musial

Pete Rose

Babe Ruth

Ted Williams

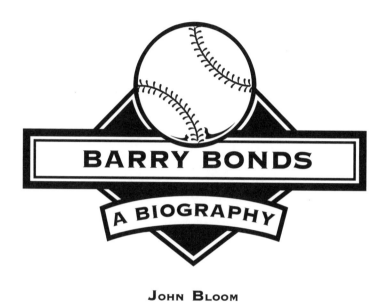

BARRY BONDS
A BIOGRAPHY

JOHN BLOOM

BASEBALL'S ALL-TIME GREATEST HITTERS

GREENWOOD PRESS
WESTPORT, CONNECTICUT • LONDON

Library of Congress Cataloging-in-Publication Data

Bloom, John, 1962–
    Barry Bonds : a biography / John Bloom.
        p. cm.—(Baseball's all-time greatest hitters)
    Includes bibliographical references and index.
    ISBN 0–313–32955–9 (alk. paper)
    1. Bonds, Barry, 1964–   2. Baseball players—United States—Biography.   I. Title.
II. Series.
    GV865.B63B56   2004
    796.357'092—dc22   2004017424

British Library Cataloguing in Publication Data is available.

Library of Congress Catalog Card Number: 2004017424
ISBN: 0–313–32955–9

First published in 2004

Greenwood Press, 88 Post Road West, Westport, CT 06881
An imprint of Greenwood Publishing Group, Inc.
www.greenwood.com

Printed in the United States of America

The paper used in this book complies with the
Permanent Paper Standard issued by the National
Information Standards Organization (Z39.48–1984).

10 9 8 7 6 5 4 3 2 1

Contents

Series Foreword   vii

Acknowledgments   xi

Chronology   xiii

Introduction   xvii

Chapter 1 ✦ In His Father's Footsteps, 1964–1986   1

Chapter 2 ✦ Stardom and Dashed Hopes in Pittsburgh, 1986–1992   17

Chapter 3 ✦ Salvaging a Franchise, 1993   31

Chapter 4 ✦ A Tarnished Image for Bonds and Baseball, 1994   39

Chapter 5 ✦ A Target of Resentment, 1995–1999   49

Chapter 6 ✦ Chasing the Babe in the House That Bonds Built,
                 2000–2001   63

Chapter 7 ✦ A Dream Come True . . . Almost, 2002   77

Chapter 8 ✦ Private Struggles and Public Images, 2003   89

Chapter 9 ✦ " 'Roid Rage"   99

Epilogue   115

Contents

Appendix: Barry Bonds' Awards and Career and Postseason Statistics   122

Selected Bibliography   125

Index   129

SERIES FOREWORD

The volumes in Greenwood's "Baseball's All-Time Greatest Hitters" series present the life stories of the players who, through their abilities to hit for average, for power, or for both, most helped their teams at the plate. Much thought was given to the players selected for inclusion in this series. In some cases, the selection of certain players was a given. **Ty Cobb, Rogers Hornsby**, and **Joe Jackson** hold the three highest career averages in baseball history: .367, .358, and .356, respectively. **Babe Ruth**, who single-handedly brought the sport out of its "Dead Ball" era and transformed baseball into a home-run hitters game, hit 714 home runs (a record that stood until 1974) while also hitting .342 over his career. **Lou Gehrig**, now known primarily as the man whose consecutive-games record Cal Ripken Jr. broke in 1995, hit .340 and knocked in more than 100 runs eleven seasons in a row, totaling 1,995 before his career was cut short by ALS. **Ted Williams**, the last man in either league to hit .400 or better in a season (.406 in 1941), is widely regarded as possibly the best hitter ever, a man whose fanatical dedication raised hitting to the level of both science and art.

Two players set career records that, for many, define the art of hitting. **Hank Aaron** set career records for home runs (755) and RBIs (2,297). He also maintained a .305 career average over twenty-three seasons, a remarkable feat for someone primarily known as a home-run hitter. **Pete Rose** had ten seasons with 200 or more hits and won three batting titles on his way to establishing his famous record of 4,256 career hits. Some critics have claimed that both players' records rest more on longevity than excellence. To that I would say there is something to be said about longevity and, in both cases, the player's excellence was the reason why he had the opportunity to keep playing, to keep tallying hits for his team. A base hit is the mark of a successful plate appearance; a home run is the apex of an at-bat. Accordingly, we could hardly have a series titled "Baseball's All-Time Greatest Hitters" without including the two men who set the career records in these categories.

Joe DiMaggio holds another famous mark: fifty-six consecutive games in which he obtained a base hit. Many have called this baseball's most unbreakable record. (The player who most closely approached that mark was Pete Rose, who hit safely in forty-four consecutive games in 1978.) In his thirteen seasons, DiMaggio hit .325 with 361 home runs and 1,537 RBIs. This means he *averaged* 28 home runs and 118 RBIs per season. MVPs have been awarded to sluggers in various years with lesser stats than what DiMaggio achieved in an "average" season.

Because **Stan Musial** played his entire career with the Cardinals in St. Louis— once considered the western frontier of the baseball world in the days before baseball came to California—he did not receive the press of a DiMaggio. But Musial compiled a career average of .331, with 3,630 hits (ranking fourth all time) and 1,951 RBIs (fifth all time). His hitting prowess was so respected around the league that Brooklyn Dodgers fans once dubbed him "The Man," a nickname he still carries today.

Willie Mays was a player who made his fame in New York City and then helped usher baseball into the modern era when he moved with the Giants to San Francisco. Mays did everything well and with flair. His over-the-shoulder catch in the 1954 World Series was perhaps his most famous moment, but his hitting was how Mays most tormented his opponents. Over twenty-two seasons the "Say Hey" kid hit .302 and belted 660 home runs.

Only four players have reached the 600-home-run milestone: Mays, Aaron, Ruth, and **Barry Bonds**, who achieved that feat in 2002. Bonds, the only active player included in this series, broke the single-season home-run record when he smashed 73 for the San Francisco Giants in 2001. In the 2002 National League Championship Series, St. Louis Cardinals pitchers were so leery of pitching to him that they walked him ten times in twenty-one plate appearances. In the World Series, the Anaheim Angels walked him thirteen times in thirty appearances. He finished the Series with a .471 batting average, an on-base percentage of .700, and a slugging percentage of 1.294.

As with most rankings, this series omits some great names. Jimmie Foxx, Tris Speaker, and Tony Gwynn would have battled for a hypothetical thirteenth volume. And it should be noted that this series focuses on players and their performance within Major League Baseball; otherwise, sluggers such as Josh Gibson from the Negro Leagues and Japan's Sadaharu Oh would have merited consideration.

There are names such as Cap Anson, Ed Delahanty, and Billy Hamilton who appear high up on the list of career batting average. However, a number of these players played during the late 1800s, when the rules of baseball were drastically different. For example, pitchers were not allowed to throw overhand until 1883, and foul balls weren't counted as strikes until 1901 (1903 in the American League). Such players as Anson and company undeniably were the stars of their day, but baseball has evolved greatly since then, into a game in which hitters must now cope with night games, relief pitchers, and split-fingered fastballs.

Ultimately, a list of the "greatest" anything is somewhat subjective, but Greenwood offers these players as twelve of the finest examples of hitters throughout history. Each volume focuses primarily on the playing career of the subject: his early years in school, his years in semi-pro and/or minor league baseball, his entrance into the majors, and his ascension to the status of a legendary hitter. But even with the greatest of players, baseball is only part of the story, so the player's life before and after baseball is given significant consideration. And because no one can exist in a vacuum, the authors often take care to recreate the cultural and historical contexts of the time—an approach that is especially relevant to the multidisciplinary ways in which sports are studied today.

Batter up.

ROB KIRKPATRICK
GREENWOOD PUBLISHING

ACKNOWLEDGMENTS

This book would not have been possible without the help and support of people who must be mentioned. I would like to thank David Steele of the *San Francisco Chronicle* and Josh Suchon of the *Oakland Tribune* for their insightful interviews and for allowing me to use their quotes for this book. Writing about the representations and meanings of a sports personality like Bonds is a complex endeavor, and I was greatly aided in this task in conversations with academic colleagues who share an interest in sports and culture. Among those who were most helpful were Amy Farrell, Michael Nevin Willard, Jason Loviglio, and George Lipsitz. I would also like to thank Patrice McDermott, the Chair of the American Studies Department at the University of Maryland at Baltimore County, for hiring me as a writer in residence, something that allowed me valuable space and time to finish this book.

I reserve a special thank-you to my brother, Jim Bloom, who has worked as a public relations and marketing executive for two Major League Baseball teams over the past decade. He was instrumental in helping me get contacts and find resources on Barry Bonds, and he was a good sparring partner as I let him know what my arguments were. My parents, Maxine and Sidney Bloom, kept my writing in high gear with their newspaper clippings from California and their gentle prodding about how the Barry Bonds book was "coming along."

My 12-year-old son, Nick, was also a source of important sports facts, insights, trivia, and opinions. At times, I felt as if he should be writing this book (but only after he finished his homework). My 7-year-old daughter, Catherine, helped me lighten up my attitude with her irreverent thoughts about Barry Bonds' physical appearance.

Finally, I would like to thank my wife, Amy Farrell, for pushing me to sign on and write this book and for supporting me in my efforts to complete it. She is the best partner in life that I could imagine.

CHRONOLOGY

1964 Barry Lamar Bonds is born on July 24. Before he comes home from the hospital, a teenage boy named Dusty Baker holds him. Twenty-nine years later, Baker becomes Bonds' manager on the San Francisco Giants.

1968 Barry's father, Bobby, is called up to play for the San Francisco Giants. He hits a grand slam in his first major league at-bat.

1968–ﾠ1974 Barry regularly travels to Candlestick Park to watch his father practice. In the clubhouse, he meets Willie Mays, who becomes his godfather.

1982 Barry graduates from Junipero Serra High School in San Mateo, California, where he played baseball, basketball, and football. On the baseball diamond, he hits .404 over three varsity seasons. After hitting .467 during his senior year, he is selected as a prep All-American. In June, he is drafted by the San Francisco Giants in the second round of the amateur draft, but Bonds ultimately decides to attend Arizona State University instead of turning pro.

1984 As a sophomore, Bonds ties a National Collegiate Athletic Association (NCAA) record for the College World Series by collecting seven consecutive hits during one stretch of the tournament.

1985 Bonds hits .347 over three seasons with Arizona State with 45 home runs and 175 runs batted in. He decides not continue into his senior year and enters the amateur draft. The Pittsburgh Pirates select Bonds as the sixth overall pick.

1986 The Pirates call up Bonds to the major leagues from their Triple-A affiliate in Hawaii. Bonds has less than one year of minor league experience. On June 4, he hits his first home run off Craig McMurtry of the Atlanta Braves in Atlanta Fulton County Stadium.

1988 Bonds marries Susann "Sun" Branco in Las Vegas. He and Sun had first met the previous year while in a Montreal bar.

1990 Bonds wins his first National League Most Valuable Player award after hitting .301 with thirty-three home runs and 104 runs batted in. He also steals fifty-two bases and scores 104 runs, helping lead the Pirates to the playoffs. Pittsburgh loses to the Cincinnati Reds in six games, and Bonds goes 3 for 18 in the Series.

1992 Bonds wins his second Most Valuable Player award with the Pittsburgh Pirates, hitting .311 with 34 home runs and 103 runs batted in. The Pirates lose in seven games to the Atlanta Braves in the National League Championship Series for the second consecutive year, this time with Bonds unable to throw out Sid Bream, who slides across home plate in the bottom of the ninth for the winning run.

1993 Bonds becomes a free agent and signs with the San Francisco Giants. The total contract, worth $43.75 million over six years, is the highest ever paid to a Major League Baseball player. Bonds wins his second consecutive Most Valuable Player (MVP) award, the third of his career, after hitting .336 with a career-high 46 home runs and 123 runs batted in.

1994 In August, Major League Baseball players go on strike, ending the season and canceling the World Series. At the time of the strike, Bonds is hitting .312 with 37 home runs. In May, he and Sun Bonds separate. They finalize their divorce on December 12. Their divorce settlement remains in court for several years.

1997 Bonds helps lead the Giants to the postseason for the first time in his career. However, he continues to suffer at the plate in the playoffs, managing only 3 hits in 12 at-bats as the Giants are swept by the eventual World Series champion, the Florida Marlins.

1998 In January, Bonds marries longtime friend Liz Watson.

2000 Bonds and the Giants go to the playoffs for the second time, and, once more, Bonds struggles with his hitting. He goes 3 for 17, and the Giants lose in four games in the divisional series to the New York Mets.

2001   Bonds hits 73 home runs in a single season, the most ever by any player in Major League Baseball history. His record shatters that set by Mark McGwire only three years earlier, which itself broke a record that had stood for thirty-seven years. As impressive as his home-run total, Bonds sets a major league record for slugging percentage with an .863 mark. He also draws 177 walks. In April, he also hits his 500th career home run off Terry Adams of the Los Angeles Dodgers. At the end of the season, he earns his fourth Most Valuable Player award. No other player has ever been voted MVP more than three times.

2002   Bonds leads the Giants to the postseason once again and this time is able to perform well at the plate. He hits three home runs and goes 5 for 17 in the opening series against the Atlanta Braves, helping the Giants win in five games. The Anaheim Angels eventually beat the Giants in seven games in the World Series, but Bonds hits a record 8 postseason home runs. He is voted MVP for a second consecutive year for the fifth time in his career after hitting .370 and earning the first batting title of his career. He also hits his 600th home run off Kip Wells of the Pittsburgh Pirates.

2003   In late August, Barry's father, Bobby, dies at the age of 57 due to complications linked to cancer. Bonds and the Giants go to the playoffs for the second consecutive year but lose to the Florida Marlins in four games. After batting .341 with 45 home runs, he is selected as the National League MVP for the third consecutive year and the sixth time in his career. In December, he is called to testify before a federal grand jury investigating BALCO (a company that provides nutritional supplements to bodybuilders and athletes) for the illegal sale and distribution of anabolic steroids. Bonds' personal trainer, Greg Anderson, is one of the central targets of the probe.

2004   In February, Greg Anderson and three others linked to BALCO are indicted on forty-two counts including illegal distribution of steroids and human growth hormones. On April 12, Bonds hits his 660th career home run off Matt Kinney of the Milwaukee Brewers, tying his godfather, Willie Mays, for third place on the all-time home-run list. He hits number 661 the next night off Ben Ford of the Brewers, taking third place for himself.

INTRODUCTION

On October 5, 2001, Barry Bonds of the San Francisco Giants stood in the batter's box at Pacific Bell Park on San Francisco's China Basin waterfront awaiting a 1–0 pitch from Chan Ho Park of the Los Angeles Dodgers. A few days earlier, Bonds had tied the single-season home-run record set by Mark McGwire of the St. Louis Cardinals, hitting his 70th home run at Houston's Enron Field. It had been a momentous season for Bonds. In April, he hit the 500th home run of his career, joining an exclusive list of players and virtually guaranteeing a future place in the Baseball Hall of Fame. By mid-August, Bonds had 50 home runs and was on pace to threaten McGwire's record. McGwire had set his mark only two years earlier by overturning Roger Maris' record of 61 home runs, which had stood for thirty-seven years. Over the last weeks of the baseball season, pitchers simply attempted to avoid Bonds. *Oakland Tribune* sports reporter Josh Suchon documented that 51 of the 64 pitches thrown to Bonds during a crucial stretch at the end of the 2001 season were balls.[1] Park's 1–0 pitch was one of the unlucky 13 that ventured into Bonds' strike zone. Instead, Bonds connected with the pitch and launched the ball 442 feet beyond home plate over the right center field fence for his 71st home run of the season.

As if that were not enough, two innings later, Bonds connected with another pitch from Park for his 72nd home run of the season, and he was still not finished. Two nights later, Bonds hit his 73rd and final home run of the season. Bonds could not fully celebrate his two home runs against Park, for the Dodgers beat the Giants in extra innings on October 5, winning by a score of 11–10 and eliminating the Giants from contention for the playoffs, yet Bonds and his fans still had a lot to cheer about. By the time the game was over, it was 12:30 in the morning, and several thousand fans lingered at the ballpark to witness the celebration of an amazing athletic accomplishment.

This was a poignant moment for Bonds. For most of his career, he had been cast as a selfish, moody, aloof, and spoiled superstar athlete. For years, national sports commentators had been taking shots at Bonds, claiming that he had a bad attitude and rude personality. Whether because of this reputation or simply because of the high salary that Bonds commanded on the modern baseball market, the Giants failed to provide a contract to Bonds during this last year of his contract with the team. At the beginning of the 2001 season, many wondered whether Bonds was worth the money that the Giants would have to spend to keep him on the team and whether he had a true desire to stay with the Giants.

By October 5, however, some of those questions had been answered. Instead of heckling, fans erupted during the postgame festivities with chants of "sign him" and "four more years."[2] Bonds, in turn, expressed his loyalty to the Bay Area and the Giants organization. "To my teammates," Bonds said in his dedication after the game, "we worked real hard, and we're going to work real hard again. I love you all very much. It's an honor to play with a bunch of guys like this behind me. I'll play for you any time, any day of the week, any hour, any year."[3] By the end of the 2002 season, Bonds was still a Giant and, at the age of 37 won the National League batting title, led his team to the World Series, and became one of only four major league players to hit at least 600 career home runs.

If that is where the road had ended for Bonds, he would have a strong case to make that he deserved the title of greatest baseball player of all time, yet, amazingly, the story of Barry Bonds' baseball career has yet to be completed. Nearing the age of 40, he is playing not only the best baseball of his career but arguably the best baseball of any player's career. He won Most Valuable Player awards in 2001 and 2002, becoming the first major leaguer to win this honor five times in his career. He followed his record-breaking home-run season of 2001 with a batting title in 2002, hitting .370. Even more impressive, Bonds had a staggering on-base percentage that same year of .582, a major league record. In 2003, he stole a base in the bottom of the 11th inning en route to scoring the winning run in a key match-up against the Los Angeles Dodgers and thus became the first major league player to steal 500 bases and hit at least 500 home runs in his career. No other player has ever hit 300 home runs and stolen 300 bases. To top it all off, he has not only been an offensive powerhouse but also earned eight Gold Glove awards en route to a fielding percentage that stood at .983 at the end of the 2002 season.

Despite his amazing accomplishments as a baseball player, Barry Bonds is often portrayed as the embodiment of everything that is wrong with the game of baseball. Sportswriters accuse him of being rude to them. Columnists insist that he is mean to fans and that he is a generally disagreeable, unpleasant, and moody person. Pulitzer Prize-winning journalist David Halberstam even made the blanket assertion that "America will never love Barry Bonds."[4] During Bonds' record-breaking 73-home-run season, *Sports Illustrated* columnist Rick Reilly wrote that Bonds' heroics on the field had not left him beloved by his teammates—"he's not even beliked."[5]

Considering Bonds' accomplishments, it is remarkable that there is such a depth of negative feeling for him by so many of the nation's elite sportswriters. Such antipathy is all the more curious when considering that, compared to other celebrated ball players, Bonds has never had a remarkably dishonorable life away from the field. In the mid-1990s, he did go through a difficult divorce that saw accusations of domestic abuse made against him. The charges were serious and included accounts of beatings. However, the allegations against him are not, unfortunately, especially uncommon for contemporary athletes, many of whom have rehabilitated their public images much more successfully than Bonds has been able to do. In fact, Bonds' negative press predates his marital troubles, going back to his earliest days as a Pittsburgh Pirate when teammate Sid Bream said that Bonds "was probably somebody that everybody in the clubhouse wanted to beat up at some point in time."[6] The negative comments continue despite the fact that, according to reporters who cover him today and even according to many of his critics, he leads a relatively conservative and family-oriented life.

The antipathy voiced by the nation's media toward Barry Bonds has, perhaps, less to do with Bonds himself and more to do with the larger expectations and ideas about sports and about baseball that are reflected and reformulated in the writing of journalists. Central to these ideas is race. Barry Bonds is not only a great baseball player but also a great African American baseball player. Since Jackie Robinson entered the major leagues in 1947, baseball writers have struggled to accept black players. Some are cast as heroes, others as villains, but almost always sports commentators cast nonwhite players as actors in some larger morality play.

To understand what Barry Bonds has meant to baseball, race is a key. Race is a reason that Barry Bonds rubs so many reporters and fans the wrong way. Not only is he proud to be black, but his blackness is a source of his confidence and energy. Bonds is, in many ways, part of African American baseball royalty. He is the son of major league great Bobby Bonds, who also played for the San Francisco Giants, and the godson of Willie Mays, who, next to Bonds, is arguably the greatest baseball player to have played in the majors. Moreover, Hall of Fame slugger Reggie Jackson is a cousin, and Dusty Baker, the most successful African American manager in major league history and the Giants skipper during the majority of Bonds' tenure with the club, was such a close friend of the Bonds family that he reportedly held Barry in his arms on the day the future slugger was born. For many white reporters and fans, such black confidence is irritating, even threatening, and smacks of arrogance, and it becomes even more problematic when placed in the context of the high salaries commanded by baseball players, the inflation in baseball ticket prices, the economic disparities that have characterized the past twenty-five years, and the economics of sports that have transformed baseball from something that many identified as a "people's game" into a corporate marketing opportunity.

This book explores the baseball career of Barry Bonds by paying attention to its paradoxes. It focuses not only upon the brilliant accomplishments of Barry Bonds the baseball player but also upon the seeming inability of so many people to accept Barry Bonds the person.

NOTES

1. Josh Suchon, *This Gracious Season: Barry Bonds and the Greatest Year in Baseball* (Winter Publications, 2002).

2. Henry Schulman, "A Day of Mixed Emotions, Uncertainty, Elimination Undermine Bonds' Joy," *San Francisco Chronicle*, October 7, 2001.

3. Ibid.

4. David Halberstam, "Why America Will Never Love Barry Bonds," ESPN.com, July 17, 2001, http://espn.go.com/page2/s/halberstam/010719.html.

5. Rick Reilly, "He Loves Himself Barry Much," *Sports Illustrated*, August 27, 2002, 102.

6. Steve Travers, *Barry Bonds: Baseball's Superman* (Champaign, IL: Sports, LLC, 2002), 51.

IN HIS FATHER'S FOOTSTEPS, 1964–1986

In May 1986, the *New York Times* reported in a short blurb on a minor league outfielder playing in Hawaii: "Barry Bonds, the son of the former major league outfielder Bobby Bonds, drove in seven runs for Hawaii on Monday with a grand slam and two singles in a Pacific Coast League game in Calgary, Alberta, that Hawaii won, 18–8."[1] Today, it seems almost quaint to think that at one time the greatest claim to fame for Barry Bonds was the fact that he was Bobby Bonds' son, but in the spring of 1986, the only thing that made Barry worthy of mention in the *New York Times* was his family tree.

Bobby Bonds was not, as his son would become, a certain Hall-of-Famer, but he was a great player about whom almost any baseball fan knew. Although Barry would excel far beyond his father's accomplishments as a baseball player, his story is still very much connected to that of Bobby Bonds. An important aspect of this connection is its relationship to African American sports history. Bobby Bonds was, in many ways, a bridge between two eras of black athletic history in the United States. When he entered professional sports in the mid-1960s, Bobby played with stars like Willie Mays, who were of the first generation to integrate Major League Baseball. As historians David Wiggins and Patrick Miller have written, African American athletes of the civil rights era were important in "richly symbolic terms." Their success and heroism created pride and "established role models for African Americans who believed that the time had come to assert their claims to *full* participation in the life of the nation."[2] Wiggins and Miller also note that by the time Bobby Bonds finished his playing career in 1981, there was a widespread sense of alienation among black athletes be-

Bonds was a star outfielder for Junipero Serra High School in San Mateo, California, between 1979 and 1982. He helped lead his high school baseball team to conference and division championships during each of his three years on the varsity squad and led his league in home runs, total bases, and stolen bases during each of these seasons as well. *Junipero Serra High School.*

cause their success on the playing field contradicted the more general condition of African Americans, who faced cuts in social programs and rollbacks of hard-won civil rights victories. Black athletes often felt a sense of betrayal and bitterness—that they were held to a different standard than white players; that they were not rewarded with front office or managerial positions once their playing days ended; that they were subject to stereotypes and negative images that highlighted their human frailties and credited their success to "natural" ability rather than to hard work and character.[3]

Bobby Bonds was born on March 15, 1946, in Riverside, California. In the late 1940s, Riverside was a rural community, but it was poised to become a suburban mecca spurred by the unprecedented industrial growth brought to the Pacific Coast during and following World War II. The war brought population and jobs to California, and Riverside benefited both directly and indirectly from this economic boom. Not only was the town transforming from a rural farm region to a residential city of suburban middle-class housing, but the state had also decided to locate one of its University of California campuses there. This new campus was part of a phenomenal expansion of the state's higher education resources under the governorship of Earl Warren, who, during his term of office, enjoyed huge budget surpluses made possible by the state's economic success.[4]

California's postwar economic boom and progressive public policies made it the envy of the nation after World War II. These circumstances have often led to assumptions that places like Riverside were relatively more progressive in their treatment of African Americans than other regions of the country during this time period.[5] After all, blacks were migrating to Southern California in record numbers during the 1940s and 1950s, seeking jobs in the emerging defense manufacturing industry and other related businesses, yet for an African American like Bobby Bonds, Riverside was not free from racial prejudice and discrimination. In fact, it had a long history of segregation that was only beginning to break down in the late 1940s and that has persisted, in many respects, to the present day.

Riverside had formally segregated schools until December 1946, just a few months after Bobby Bonds was born. It changed this policy only because of the threat of legal action, which caused the local school board to end long-held segregation policies against blacks and Mexican Americans.[6] However, Riverside continued to be a segregated community even after formal laws preventing integration were overturned. In 1968, University of California—Riverside professor Thomas Carter did a study of a place he called "Alphatown," which greatly resembled Riverside in size and location. His qualitative survey focused upon the dramatic de facto residential and educational segregation that characterized

"Alphatown," where whites interacted with few Mexican Americans or blacks in schools or in neighborhoods, and where people of color constituted a disproportionately high number of the unemployed. In interviews, young Anglo residents revealed deep-seated fears about attending school or playing sports with members of either the Mexican American or African American communities.[7]

For young African Americans like Bobby Bonds, sports were an important way to express dignity and self-worth within this segregated community. This was particularly true after World War II with the integration of professional sports, the boom in popularity of spectator sports, and the increased recognition of athletes and of sports teams themselves through television. The year Bobby Bonds was born, there were no blacks in Major League Baseball and only twelve major league teams, while televised sports did not really exist. However, by the time Bobby was 12 years old in 1958, young African Americans could hang their aspirations on numerous black athletes—most of them male—who were playing at both the collegiate and professional levels. For the first time, many African Americans could look at sports as more than an activity to build community spirit and enhance local African American institutions—they could see it as something that might bring individual wealth, status, and success.[8]

Barry, the eldest of Patricia and Bobby Bonds' four children, was born on July 24, 1964, in Riverside, where his ties to this tradition began. Bobby Bonds provided his son not only with a family name connected to baseball history but with other ties that linked Barry to the new African American sports tradition that was emerging after World War II. Dusty Baker, a close friend of the elder Bonds, would later play for the Atlanta Braves and Los Angeles Dodgers. Baker not only would become, arguably, the most successful African American manager in major league history but would do so as the manager of Barry Bonds' San Francisco Giants. Barry's aunt Rosie Bonds in Riverside held the U.S. women's record in the eighty-meter hurdles and was on the U.S. Olympic Team for the Tokyo games in 1964, the year Barry was born.

When Bobby began his career with San Francisco, the Giants were still known as a pioneering team with regard to the integration of baseball. Under the ownership of Horace Stoneham in New York in the 1950s, the Giants signed some of the greatest African American players of their era, including Willie Mays and Monte Irvin. Later, the Giants would be among the first teams to make a foray into the Dominican Republic, signing the superstar Alou brothers (Jose, Matty, and future manager Felipe) and Juan Marichal.[9]

Barry would spend time with his father in the Giants locker room and on the field during batting practice. There he met Willie Mays, one of the greatest Major League Baseball players ever. Mays, as many fans know, became Bonds' godfather. Mays told reporter David Grann that Barry "was always watching me . . . to take my glove."[10] Bobby Bonds and Willie Mays shared the outfield. Also a distant cousin of Hall of Fame slugger Reggie Jackson, Barry Bonds told Grann, "I was born into this game."[11]

Bobby Bonds' fourteen-year major league career was marked by high hopes and disappointments. Combining speed and power, he broke into the major leagues during the 1968 season with the San Francisco Giants. While hitting .370 with Phoenix of the Pacific Coast League, he got the call to the majors for a June series against the Dodgers. In his first major league at bat, Bonds hit a grand slam home run to help the Giants beat their rivals from Los Angeles 9 to 0.[12] Known as well for his acrobatic catches and strong throwing arm, it was not long before sportswriters in the Bay Area began to label Bobby Bonds the "next Willie Mays."

Bonds would go on to do great things. He became one of the few players ever to hit over 300 home runs (332 total) and steal over 300 bases (461 total) during a major league career; he won three Gold Glove awards; he led the league in runs in 1969 and 1973; and he was the 1973 All Star Game's Most Valuable Player. However, he became better known as a journeyman by the end of his career. After the Giants traded him to the New York Yankees for Bobby Mercer in 1975, Bonds played for seven different teams in seven seasons. Bonds would later express bitterness over the way his career turned out, something that sportswriters sometimes characterized as whining. Yet it is also important to place Bonds' feelings within the larger context of alienation that black athletes expressed during this era, a time when the optimism that had followed Jackie Robinson's integration into Major League baseball had begun to fade.

As much as sports were providing blacks with avenues toward success, the sports industry was still controlled by whites and began to look increasingly like a system of white owners who exploited black talent. Even the Giants, once the model of integration, had changed direction. Between the time that he signed with the club and the time that they traded him away, San Francisco had unloaded an All-Star team of color that included Willie Kirkland, José Tartabul, Manny Mota, Felipe and Matty Alou, José Cardenal, José Pagan, Orlando Cepeda, George Foster, Willie Mays, Ed Figueroa, Willie McCovey, and Bonds himself. As baseball historian Steve Treder pointed out, in each case, the Giants chose to receive a white player as compensation.[13]

Despite the many moves that his father would make around the major leagues in the following years—to New York, Anaheim, Chicago (White Sox), Texas, Cleveland, St. Louis, and back to Chicago (Cubs)—Barry Bonds spent most of his childhood in the affluent suburb of San Carlos, south of San Francisco. Unlike the Riverside area in which his father was raised, San Carlos was predominantly white. In this respect, Barry Bonds might be seen as part of a first generation as well—the first generation of African American children born and raised within the affluence and atmosphere of sports celebrity and success.

Growing up with a father who was a famous baseball player also had its downside for Barry. "You don't know who your friends are at times . . . you don't know if they want to be your friend because you're the son of Bobby Bonds." For many years after his father had been traded to the Yankees, Bobby was absent from his family home. Barry has lamented that his father was never at his Little League games and that only his mother would show up at these events. Bobby claimed to have watched his son play while the father sat in his car, so as not to attract attention, but Barry says that he never saw him.[14] "My father and I were never really close when I was growing up," according to Barry, "because he was never around. I wanted my dad at my Little League games, because everybody else's parents were there. My parents were not there, just my mom."[15]

Toward the end of his career, the elder Bonds had a problem with alcohol that added to Barry's sense of disengagement from his father. When Bobby was arrested for drunk driving, the Bonds family had to deal not only with their father's problem but also with the media attention that followed the children to school. Bobby's drinking, and the publicity it generated, was something that served as a source of humiliation for Barry. Fans would use it to taunt the young star when he first played as a collegiate and professional baseball player.

The relationship between the press and Bobby Bonds was a strained one from early on in his career. Although he was a strong performer, he was not living up to his billing as the "next Willie Mays." As Bobby Bonds would later put it, "anything I did that wasn't what Willie Mays did meant I never lived up to my potential."[16] Adding to this, Bobby Bonds was one of the first players to take advantage of "free agency" in Major League Baseball. Until the mid-1970s, Major League Baseball players were tied for life to the teams with which they first signed unless they were traded. Their obligations to their team remained in place even after the terms of their contracts had expired. In 1974, the U.S. Supreme Court ruled this part of a player's major league contract, known as the "reserve clause," unconstitutional. Players whose contracts had expired were now free to negotiate with any team they chose. The first free agents were able to get much higher salaries after they were given the freedom to negotiate with more than one team, yet many players paid a heavy price to their reputations. When players like Bobby Bonds sought better contracts and working conditions in the free agent market, they were shredded by sports reporters and portrayed as traitors who betrayed not only their teams and fans but also the game of baseball itself.

Growing up in an environment in which his father was a constant source of material for the negative sentiments of sportswriters gave Barry Bonds a unique insight into professional athletics. From an early stage in his career, he did not trust the press and kept them at a distance. In many ways, this was a product of his father's experiences. In a 2003 interview with the author, Barry Bonds biographer Josh Suchon explained the origins of Bonds' distrust of the media.

> He . . . believes that . . . the press never gave his father a fair shake. He always felt that from the time that he was in high school. So he distrusted the media before the media even started writing bad things about him. I think that's an important thing to understand in the Barry Bonds relationship with the media. I remember when I was doing the research for my book. I found a quote, I think it was from '88 or '89 . . . so this was before Barry became the MVP Barry Bonds. This was when he was still an up and coming player trying to establish himself. And he had a quote that said, "the media never did my father right, why would I expect the media to do me right." I think that's an important lesson to know about Barry.[17]

Indeed, Barry's childhood was not only marked by athletic success, it was also one lived in tension with the media spotlight. Barry Bonds was already being labeled a great all-around athlete even before he began his famed high school sports career at Junipero Serra High School in San Mateo, California. There is a widely circulated legend about a young Barry Bonds, living in Riverside in the years before he moved to Northern California, shattering windows at his house while playing whiffle-ball in the back yard. He did this so many times that his mother, Pat, was a familiar customer at the local glass store.

Although interested and active in sports, Bonds was also very private and close to his mother. Despite the often reported stories that Bonds would hang around the Giants clubhouse while his father practiced, Bonds recalled enjoying time at home with his mother far more. "I'd rather watch my mom put her makeup on," he has said in interviews. "Or put on a wig and dance with her; . . . I didn't like my dad that much. We didn't become close until I was in college." Childhood friend Bob McKercher remembers that Bonds was like many other kids in the neighborhood. "We were into water-balloon fights, we played baseball, basketball, football. We loved music and liked to dance. We went to the movies. Every Friday night from sixth to eighth grade we went ice-skating. He was just a typical kid."[18]

Serra High, as it is known in the San Francisco Bay Area, was a perfect school for such a talented player. It is a parochial school that has earned a reputation as the training ground for future great athletes. Football great Lynn Swan and baseball star Jim Fregosi preceded Barry Bonds there, and Super Bowl Most

Valuable Player Tom Brady and baseball star Gregg Jefferies would follow him. Bonds tried to take advantage of all that the school offered athletically. Like his father, he played more than one sport. In football, he was a respected wide receiver, and in basketball, he was a varsity starter and first team all conference as a senior. According to Bonds, "I played every sport! Every sport, every season, anything I could play, I'd play!"[19] As one might expect, however, it was in baseball that Bonds really stood out, displaying his trademark combination of speed, defense, and hitting ability.

Biographies of Bonds paint him as a less than stellar student at Serra High School, working hard enough to get by but putting most of his real effort into sports. Averaging grades in the "C" range, Bonds drew the ire of his biology teacher. According to Randy Vogel, the Serra High School director of admissions, the teacher grew so frustrated that he issued a warning. "One day the teacher decided he'd try to motivate Barry. . . . So he told him, 'Barry, you better get yourself in gear because baseball will never get you anywhere.'" According to legend, the teacher who made this comment is so embarrassed that he refuses to identify himself to this day.[20]

Recalling his high school career, Bonds has downplayed his superstar status, saying that he was not really the best hitter on his team. "It depends if you go by at-bats. Some of my friends said that they hit higher than me, but they may have had less at-bats than I did. There were guys who hit for a higher average, but we all hit .400 or something like that. My buddy might have hit .445 and I hit .430."[21] His former teammates, however, say that Bonds was so fast, he could steal bases standing up.[22] Bonds started by playing on the freshman team, but he skipped up to varsity for his sophomore year, and he made an early impact, earning second team all conference honors. During his junior and senior years, he was first-team all conference and was named a prep All-American in 1982, when he also served as team captain. He still holds a high place in the record books at Serra. His career batting average of .404 stands as seventh among players at his former high school. Bonds also is tied for the school record for most runs in a game, scoring four against San Carlos in 1980; four against Archbishop Riordan in 1981; and four against El Camino in 1981. He still holds the school record for having achieved this milestone three times in his high school career. He helped lead his high school baseball team to conference and division championships during each of his three years on the varsity squad and led his league in home runs, total bases, and stolen bases during each of these seasons as well.[23]

According to his father, "he could hit the ball as far as anybody."[24] This is not just the perspective of a proud father. Even in high school, friends remember that Bonds could hit tape-measure home-run shots. In a playoff game against

El Camino High School's fastest thrower in 1981, Bob McKercher recalled that Bonds hit a ball over a 405-foot sign in right center field. According to McKercher, "It didn't just clear the fence; it went halfway up the tree behind it. It was like a bullet." When scouts first came to one of Bonds' high school games and convinced the Serra head coach to let Bonds use a wooden bat for his first time at the plate, Bonds hit a home run. Joe Kmak, who played with Bonds on the Serra High School team, remembers Bonds' exceptional hitting ability. "It seemed like when he wanted a hit, he'd get one. . . . When the focus was there, he knew he'd get a hit. And the greater the competition, the greater his focus."[25]

However, power hitting was not the only connection between Bonds' adolescence and his future as an adult. At Serra many first labeled Barry Bonds as someone with a bad attitude. According to Bonds, this was largely the result of resentment. He remembers, "Everything was easy for me, all sports, when I was a kid. I'd work half as hard as other kids did and I was better. Why work when I had so much ability? Some other kids were jealous." McKercher also thinks that Bonds himself was feeling increasingly troubled as a high school student. As Bobby Bonds would get traded from team to team, Barry saw less of his father. Each trade seemed to take a toll on Barry. "It was like his dad wasn't wanted. . . . You see that, and it lingers. You see your dad go from San Francisco to New York to Anaheim to Texas to Cleveland to Chicago . . . that can take a toll on you."[26]

As his father was increasingly absent, Bonds looked to his coaches as male authority figures. Kevin Donahue, the basketball coach at Serra, recalled talking to Bonds about his problems at home. "Barry spent a lot of time in my office talking about problems, most of them the typical problems teenagers have. He was under a microscope because of who his dad was. People always expected him to perform well. When he made a mistake, people tended to be more critical of him." Russ Bertetta, Bonds' English and history teacher, also remembered that high school was a difficult emotional time for Bonds. "He's basically the same person now that he was in high school, but everything's so magnified. He was a pretty sensitive guy. He's still that way but has a harder shell. When he's in a good mood, he's a great guy, and it was the same in high school. When he wasn't in a good mood, you didn't want to be around him."[27]

Even though Bonds had a spectacular senior year in 1982, earning a .462 batting average, which stands as the eighth best season total in his high school's history, he was denied the Most Valuable Player award. According to former high school teammate Dave Canziani, "that had to do with the fact that Barry was perceived even then to be cocky and arrogant. . . . He clearly deserved the award."[28]

The San Francisco Giants drafted Bonds out of high school in 1982, but he and the team could not come to terms on a contract. In a dispute that seems almost comical today, the Giants declined Bonds' request for $75,000, refusing to go any higher than $70,000. The next time that San Francisco would have an opportunity to sign Bonds to a contract, there would be several more zeros added to their salary offer.

Instead of going to the minor leagues, Bonds elected to attend college. He had been offered several scholarships and finally decided on Arizona State University, where his distant cousin Reggie Jackson had starred for the Sun Devils years before. During the years that Bonds was in college, the University of Southern California was probably the top baseball program on the West Coast, featuring two future major league players who are certain Hall of Famers—Randy Johnson and Mark McGwire. Yet Arizona State's head baseball coach Jim Brock, known as a great recruiter, was able to lure Bonds to Tempe. His presence on the Sun Devils squad helped to propel them to the highest levels of college baseball. At Arizona State, Bonds played on teams that featured such future major league players as Mike Devereaux, Chris Beasley, Oddibe McDowell, and Doug Henry.

Bonds helped take the Sun Devils to the College World Series in 1983 and 1984. Bonds developed even more as a baseball player who could run and hit for power while at Arizona State. Once timed at 9.5 seconds in the 100-yard dash, he also led his team with a .568 slugging percentage in 1983. His 11 home runs that year remain a school record for freshmen. During the NCAA regional playoffs that same year, he hit a home run over Arizona State's infamous "Green Monster" in center field, becoming one of only eighteen players since 1972 to do so. In that same game, he hit 3 for 3, scoring 4 runs and batting in 4 more. His performance in the tournament earned him the 1983 West II Regional Most Valuable Player award.[29]

Bonds continued to develop as a power hitter in college. The extent to which Bonds was able to do so is something often overlooked by his critics. Particularly as Bonds became shadowed by rumors linking him to the use of steroids later in his major league career, many saw his high home-run totals in the early 2000s as a departure from his early reputation for speed and defense. Bonds' detractors often point to his relatively thin physique as a young player and note how much this differs from the muscular body that he would develop later in life. Yet his college career shows how Bonds had a reputation for power even before he became a professional player. Former major league pitcher Jack McDowell, writing for *Yahoo! Sports*, recalled facing Bonds while in college.

> When Bonds was a junior at Arizona State, I was a freshman at Stanford. The flagpole behind the centerfield fence at Stanford's Sunken

Diamond stands probably 60 feet beyond the 400-foot mark in center. That would be the same flagpole a Bonds home run reached after connecting with one of my fastballs in 1985. I faced Bonds again later in the year, and he hit a home run at Arizona State's Packard Stadium into the street beyond right field. . . . The story was the same when we faced each other in spring training while Bonds was a Pirate and I was with the White Sox—a homer every time I threw against him. My point is: home runs are not new to this guy. And milestone after milestone shows that he has become a more prolific power hitter since the days when our paths crossed.[30]

In 1984, Bonds continued to excel at the plate and on the base paths. He hit .360 with 11 home runs and stole 30 bases in 45 attempts. Counting his home runs, 33 of Bonds' 93 hits that year were for extra bases. He also batted in 55 runs that season, including six game-winning hits, and grounded into only one double play during the entire season. His shining moment in college came that year in the College World Series, where he tied an NCAA record with seven hits in seven consecutive at-bats. For his performance he earned ESPN's amateur athlete of the week award.[31]

As in high school, Bonds sometimes had trouble getting along with teammates. The baseball team's head coach, Jim Brock, was able to develop a strong, affectionate relationship with Bonds, but even he recalled that the superstar outfielder was often rude. "I liked the hell out of Barry Bonds," Brock said before he died in 1994 of liver cancer. "Unfortunately, I never saw a teammate care about him. He bragged about the money he turned down, and he popped off about his dad. I don't think he ever figured what to do to get people to like him." Bonds drove a fancy black Trans Am around campus, and some expressed the desire to slash his tires.[32]

Bonds entered his junior year at Arizona State hopeful that his team would take the tough southern division title of the Pac-10 and advance to the College World Series once more. However, the Sun Devils were placed on probation that year for violating NCAA rules after a Pac-10 investigation uncovered five players who had received excessive financial aid. As a consequence, the conference stripped the Sun Devils of their 1984 conference title, took away scholarships, and barred four players from competing during the first part of the 1985 season. Even more importantly, the Sun Devils were declared ineligible for postseason play, meaning that they would not be able to try again for the College World Series title.[33]

Nevertheless, Bonds would have his best season at the plate in 1985. He hit 23 home runs, which still ranks as the third best single-season home-run total in school history. His .368 batting average was his best in college, and he would drive in 66 runs that year, earning *Sporting News* All-America honors. Despite the team's exclusion from postseason play, Bonds led the Sun Devils to the Pac-10 Southern Division championship game against Stanford. They ended up losing the game 15–10, but only after Bonds hit a two-run homer in the eighth inning.

After his junior season, Bonds elected to put his name into the professional baseball draft once more. This time, the Pittsburgh Pirates picked him up, selecting him as the sixth player in the first round. As a pro in the minor leagues, Bonds did not take long to make a big impact. Playing for Prince William of the class A Carolina League, Bonds hit .299 in 71 games. He showed once more that he could combine speed and power, belting 33 extra-base hits, 13 of which were home runs, and stealing 15 bases. Howie Haak, the chief scout for the Pirates, said that Bonds was better than Darryl Strawberry was at the same age. In the Venezuelan winter league All Star Game that following December, Bonds stole the spotlight, hitting a triple and a single and scoring twice to lead the foreign All-Star team to victory over the Venezuelan All-Stars.[34]

Meanwhile, the comparisons with his father were beginning for Barry. A Pirate spokesman told reporters, "If Barry is even close to being the player his father was, we've hit the jackpot."[35] The Pirates invited Bonds to spring training camp in Florida to begin the 1986 season. Pittsburgh featured a young team with up-and-coming stars Andy Van Slyke and Sid Bream. Despite their potential, they had little to show for the talent that they were developing, finishing the 1985 season with a pathetic record of 57 wins and 104 losses. The club rested many of its hopes for an eventual turnaround on Bonds.

Symbolizing their investment in their new star, the club gave a nonroster Bonds the number 7 for training camp. According to the team's acting public relations director Greg Johnson, the number was a reference to another secret weapon with a similar last name, "agent 007," James Bond.[36] However, many also worried about the consequences of bringing him up to the major-league level too soon. "He's a great talent," said former Pirates manager Chuck Tanner, "but what you have to avoid with young players like Bonds is rushing them to the big leagues. . . . You don't want to get them up here too quick and have them face a Dwight Gooden and wreck their confidence."[37]

Instead of allowing Bonds to skip directly from single A ball to the major leagues, the Pirates management decided to test him by assigning their future star to their AAA affiliate in Hawaii. There, Bonds proved once again that he could exceed expectations. In his 44 games before being called up, he hit .311. Seven of his hits were over the fence, and he knocked in 37 runs.[38]

Meanwhile, the Pirates were beginning their 1986 campaign where their 1985 season had ended. After being swept by Pete Rose and the Cincinnati Reds toward the end of May, Pittsburgh's record fell to 15 wins and 22 losses, a season low. What's more, they had won only 5 of their 19 home games that season. Manager Jim Leyland had clearly seen enough and could wait no longer. After the last game of the series, Leyland let his frustrations out on his team in what the Associated Press described as a "15-minute, obscenity-laced tirade." After lambasting his players, Leyland told reporters, "We've called up Barry Bonds from Hawaii and he's going to lead off and play center field . . . somebody's going to have to sit down and I don't care if their feelings are hurt. This is the major leagues and you've got to perform."[39]

It is little wonder that the struggling Pirates felt that it was Bonds' time, despite the fact that their prospect had played less than one year of Minor League Baseball. While opponents were victimizing the major league club, Barry Bonds and his teammates in Hawaii were scorching the Pacific Coast League. In May, Bonds drove in seven runs in an 18–8 rout of Calgary, hitting a grand slam and two singles, and, just a few nights before Bonds was called up, Hawaii beat the Phoenix Firebirds (the Giants AAA affiliate) by the score of 31 to 5. Bonds had what was, amazingly, the only home run of the game.[40] According to legend, Syd Thrift, the Pittsburgh general manager, had come to watch Bonds play at Phoenix. During batting practice, Thrift watched the young left-handed batter pull five home runs over the right field wall. He complimented Bonds on his impressive feat but said that he wanted to see some hit over the left field wall. Bonds proceeded to do just that, turning to Thrift and saying, "How's that?" Barry Bonds would never take another batting practice in the minor leagues.[41]

On May 30, 1986, Bonds put on the Pittsburgh Pirates uniform for the first time, donning number 24, the same number that his godfather, Willie Mays, had worn playing for the Giants. In his first game against Dodgers pitcher Rick Honeycutt, Bonds got his first base hit. Five days later, against Atlanta Braves right-hander Craig McMurtry, Bonds hit the first of his over 600 career home runs. The player whom the United Press had called a "carbon copy of his dad" in December was on his way to making his own impression as one of the all-time great players in Major League Baseball.

NOTES

1. "In Father's Footsteps," *New York Times*, May 7, 1986, D28.

2. David K. Wiggins and Patrick B. Miller, *The Unlevel Playing Field: A Documentary History of the African American Experience in Sport* (Urbana: University of Illinois Press, 2003), 206.

3. Ibid., 318.

4. John Aubrey Douglass, "Earl Warren's New Deal: Economic Transition, Postwar Planning, and Higher Education in California," *Journal of Policy History* 12, no. 4, 2000, 473–512.

5. See Travers, *Barry Bonds*, 27.

6. Lester Phillips, "Segregation in Education: A California Case Study," *Phylon (1940–1956)* 10, no. 4, 4th Quarter 1949, 407–413.

7. Thomas P. Carter and Nathaniel Hickerson, "A California Citizens' Committee Studies Its Schools and *De Facto* Segregation," *Journal of Negro Education* 37, no. 2, 1968, 98–105.

8. See Conclusion to Rob Ruck, *Sandlot Seasons: Sport in Black Pittsburgh* (Urbana: University of Illinois Press, 1987), 170–210.

9. Steve Treder, "A Legacy of What-Ifs: Horace Stoneham and the Integration of the Giants," *Nine* 10, no. 2, 71–101; Rob Ruck, *The Tropics of Baseball: Baseball in the Dominican Republic* (Lincoln: University of Nebraska Press, 1998).

10. David Grann, "Slugging It Out," *Observer* (London), October 6, 2002, 52.

11. Ibid.

12. Travers, *Barry Bonds*, 28.

13. Treder, "A Legacy of What-Ifs," 71–101.

14. David Grann, "Baseball without Metaphor," *New York Times Magazine*, September 1, 2002, 36.

15. Grann, "Slugging It Out," 52.

16. Grann, "Baseball Without Metaphor," 36.

17. Josh Suchon, interview with author, May 15, 2003.

18. Mike DiGiovanna, "Barry Bonds Biography," http://www.allstarz.org/~barrybonds/bio.htm.

19. "When I Was a Kid: An Interview with San Francisco Giants Barry Bonds," *Junior Baseball*, http://www.juniorbaseball.com/wheniwasakid/bonds.shtml.

20. DiGiovanna, "Barry Bonds Biography."

21. Ibid.

22. Grann, "Baseball without Metaphor," 36.

23. Official Web site of the Arizona State Sun Devils, http://thesundevils.com/sports/m-basebl/spec-rel/bonds-watch.html; "Serra High School Alumni Hall of Fame," http://www.Serrahs.com/Alumni/Hall_of_Fame/1992/1992.html.

24. Dave Anderson, "Sports of the Times," *New York Times*, October 10, 1990, A29.

25. Grann, "Baseball without Metaphor," 36.

26. DiGiovanna, "Barry Bonds Biography."

27. Ibid.

28. Ibid.

29. Official Web site of the Arizona State Sun Devils, http://thesundevils.ocsn.com/sports/m-basebl/specrel/bonds-watch.html.

30. Jack McDowell, "Bonds Is One of a Kind," *Yahoo! Sports*, April 8, 2004, http://sports.yahoo.com/mlb/news;_ylc=X3oDMTBpMGlxY3AxBF9Tazk10DyxNzc3.

31. Official Web site of the Arizona State Sun Devils.

32. DiGiovanna, "Barry Bonds Biography."

33. Bob Cuomo, "Pacific 10 Southern Division Preview Penalties Spur Arizona State, Coach Says," *Los Angeles Times*, February 6, 1985.

34. Winter Baseball Roundup, United Press International, December 11, 1985.

35. Ibid.

36. Sports News, Associated Press, February 28, 1986.

37. Sports News, Associated Press, March 3, 1986.

38. Sports News, Associated Press, May 25, 1986.

39. Ibid.

40. Sports News, Associated Press, May 23, 1986.

41. Grann, "Slugging It Out," 52.

The Pittsburgh Pirates drafted Bonds in the 1985 amateur free-agent draft. Called up in May 1986, he struggled during his first four years but in 1990 led the league with a .565 slugging percentage and helped lead his team to the playoffs, winning his first of two Most Valuable Player awards while with the Pirates. However, in three postseason appearances with Pittsburgh, Bonds struggled at the plate and developed a reputation for poor clutch hitting in October. *National Baseball Hall of Fame Library, Cooperstown, N.Y.*

STARDOM AND DASHED HOPES
IN PITTSBURGH, 1986–1992

In 1986, Barry's rookie year with the Pittsburgh Pirates, the memory of Bobby Bonds was still fresh in the minds of many baseball fans. Sportswriters openly wondered if the younger Bonds would fulfill the potential that seemed to slip by his father, and, in many respects, the memory of his father would haunt Barry Bonds. Over the next few years, Bonds is remembered for some spectacular seasons in which he helped lead the Pirates from one of the worst teams in baseball to one that many considered the best, yet he also had moments of disappointment, particularly in the postseason, that led sportswriters to suggest that underperformance was somehow a family trait.

Barry Bonds did not like the ubiquitous references to his father by sportswriters whenever they seemed to write about him, yet the father–son baseball tradition was too much for journalists to ignore, and to the young Bonds, it seemed that his every accomplishment was framed in terms of his father's career. This was even true of the day that Barry hit his first major league home run, when the *Washington Post* noted in their "Stat of the Day" that two other major league prodigies—Bob Boone (son of Ray Boone) and Roy Smalley (son of Roy Smalley Sr.)—also hit home runs.[1] Writers referred to Barry as "Bobby's Son" and noted that "following his father's footsteps around the baseball diamond hasn't been the easiest thing in the world for Barry Bonds."[2] When he performed well in a game, they speculated that some older players "may have thought they were watching Bobby Bonds."[3] Even more infuriating to the young star, sportswriters would mistakenly call him "Bobby" in postgame interview sessions early in his career, something that served as a constant irritant to the young star.

San Francisco Chronicle columnist David Steele began his career with the *New York Post* in 1988. While covering the New York Mets, Steele saw a lot of Bonds and notes that reporters would often make this mistake and that it was clearly something that Bonds found insulting. "One of the things about Barry at the time was that he really kind of had to fight for his own identity because he was still largely known as Bobby Bonds' son. . . . Almost every place he went, every encounter he had, either with fans or the media or somebody, there was either going to be a reference to him being Bobby's son . . . or somebody would mistakenly call him Bobby."4

To make matters worse, Bonds joined a Pirates team that seemed to be going nowhere. They finished the 1986 season in last place with a record of 64 wins and 98 losses, 44 games behind Division Champion New York. That year, the Pirates were ranked 11th out of 12 National League clubs in team batting average, and Bonds' own performance at the plate did not help. In contrast to his stellar spring in the minor leagues, he hit only .223 with 16 home runs and 48 runs batted in during his first big league season in 1986.

Many of the names that fans would associate with the great Pirates teams of the early 1990s had not joined the club when Bonds was first called up to Pittsburgh. Ace pitcher Doug Drabek was a rookie with the New York Yankees in 1986. Future star Andy Van Slyke, who would join Bonds in the Pittsburgh outfield, did not come over to the Pirates from St. Louis until the 1987 season. Perhaps most importantly, Bobby Bonilla, who rounded out the Pirates outfield and came to be known as Bonds' soul mate on the team, joined the squad only in midseason after being traded from the Chicago White Sox. The only player of stature already on the Pirates was slugger Sid Bream, who in subsequent years made it clear that he greatly disliked Bonds from the moment that the young outfielder stepped into the Pirates clubhouse.5

Over the next three seasons, Bonds and the Pirates showed signs of improvement, even flashes of brilliance. The outfield of Andy Van Slyke, Bobby Bonilla, and Bonds developed into one of the best in the majors. When the 1987 season began, some questioned whether Syd Thrift had been too hasty in his decision to call Barry Bonds up to the majors and make him a regular at the age of 21. In 1987, however, Bonds seemed to break through. Although he wanted to hit later in the batting order, Pirates manager Jim Leyland decided to position him as a leadoff hitter, and this decision seemed to be justified. Displaying the speed and power that would become one of his trademarks, he hit 25 home runs while stealing 32 bases. Bonds continued to improve in 1988, leading his team in a midseason run toward National League East powerhouse New York. "I've been criticized for three years for batting him leadoff," said Leyland, "but he's hitting over .300, his on-base percentage is over .400, and he's leading the league in runs scored . . . I like that quick thunder he gives us at the top of the lineup. To me, that's a pretty good leadoff man. The average fan doesn't know how much pressure it is on the opposing pitcher when he knows one mistake means he's behind 1–0 at the start of the game."[6]

For his part, Bonds accepted his role in the Pirates line-up. "Hitting .300 to me means that I'm doing my job, getting on base, so Bobby and Andy can drive me in. That's what I'm supposed to do in this offense." In those early years, Bonds did not really see himself as a player who supplied power to the line-up. "If I hit 30 homers every year, if I was a threat to hit a homer every time like Darryl Strawberry is, then I could say I was a home run hitter. That's kind of tough. I'm satisfied to keep doing what I've been doing, hit 20–25 homers a year, if I keep doing the other things."[7]

In fifteen years, this same Barry Bonds brashly promised to "wipe out" Babe Ruth's home-run record. As he stated in 1988, however, his role on the Pirates was not to drive in runs but to get on base, and he did that effectively. "People keep asking me when he's going to become a great player," said Leyland; "to me, he's pretty good right now." Bonds finished the 1988 season with a .283 batting average, a .368 on-base percentage, and 24 home runs.

When looking back at that time from a later date, however, Bonds recalled that he did not like batting leadoff. In a 1999 interview with the *Sporting News*, Bonds said, "I wasn't comfortable leading off. Before coming to the big leagues, I was never a leadoff hitter in Little League or at any point . . . I was frustrated because I was in a lot of situations with two outs. . . . The pitcher (wasn't getting on base). I just felt I could do more, and I think I pressed in the leadoff spot to prove that I could do more. I was always wishing that I was in the (fourth or fifth spot in the lineup)."[8]

In 1989, however, Bonds dropped back down to .248, and the Pirates fortunes also seemed to ride a roller coaster that paralleled Bonds' struggles at the plate. In 1988, the team finished 10 games over the .500 mark, good enough for second place in the National League East, yet 1989 seemed almost like a repeat of Bonds' rookie year as the Bucs mustered a record of only 74 wins and 88 losses, 19 games behind the division-winning Cubs.

During the 1989 season, Bonds showed flashes of the brilliance that he would display later in his career. On July 5, he hit a home run that made him and his father the all-time leaders of father–son home runs at 408 (beating out Yogi and Dale Berra, along with Gus and Buddy Bell, both tied at 407). On his 25th birthday that year, he went 3 for 3 against the Dodgers, including a home run and 3 runs scored, leading his team to a 7–4 victory. To top it all off, Bonds made a spectacular catch in left field with 2 outs and 2 on for the Dodgers in the ninth to end the game. However, Barry Bonds still was struggling in 1989, going into this game hitting only .242. By the end of the 1989 season, Bonds had a career average of only .103 with runners in scoring position in the late innings of a game, the lowest that had ever been documented by the Elias Sports Bureau.[9] Pirates manager Jim Leyland felt that Bonds was pressing too hard and that he needed to be more confident at the plate. After Bonds' birthday performance against the Dodgers, Leyland said,

> Sure, you get frustrated as a manager when you see a player with that kind of talent not doing what he's capable of doing. Barry gets frustrated. Sometimes when I sit and talk to him he gets frustrated. But he's a hell of a player, and what he's got to stop doing is getting down on himself. . . . When he's focused in, he's capable of doing anything. You sit there as a manager and think, "What can I do to help him?" These young guys don't like to hear about the older players, might not care about them, but the great hitters—Rod Carew, Pete Rose— never gave up on an at-bat. This is what we keep preaching to the kids, don't get down on yourself and give that at-bat away. If Pete Rose got five hits in a game, he wanted six. That's the way Barry's got to be.[10]

As the 1990 season began, rumors began to circulate that the Pirates might be interested in trading Bonds.[11] The Pirates refused to concede to demands by their inconsistent leadoff hitter for a better contract. When the case went to arbitration, Bonds lost.

Bonds responded by saying that the rumors about being traded did not bother him, and he came out of spring training ready to prove it. In the first series of the season, Pittsburgh took on their division rivals, the New York Mets. In the final game of the set, Bonds drove in 3 runs, threw Darryl Strawberry out at the plate, stole a base, and caught a ball against the outfield wall. His performance helped the Pirates win 2 out of 3 against New York.

The opening series against the Mets turned out to be a harbinger of things to come. The Pirates finished the 1990 season with a record of 95 wins and 67 losses, good enough for the National League Eastern Division Championship and a chance to play the Cincinnati Reds for the National League pennant. Doug Drabek had one of the best seasons a pitcher could hope for, winning 22 and losing only 6 with a 2.76 earned-run average. Bonds had a tremendous season as well, getting selected for the All Star Game for the first time and ending the season hitting .301 with 33 home runs and 52 stolen bases. As his father had done five times before him, Bonds joined the rare list of players to hit over 30 home runs and steal over 30 bases. As his father was never able to do, however, Bonds won the National League Most Valuable Player award by the Baseball Writers Association of America.

Bobby Bonds was proud of his son, but the award also recalled bitter memories. The elder Bonds nearly won the MVP award in 1973, when he hit 39 home runs, stole 43 bases, drove in 96 runs, and hit .283 only to finish third, behind Pete Rose. "I thought I should have won the M.V.P. that year. . . . The *Sporting News* named me its player of the year. . . . They gave me a big plaque, but I never put it up in the house. I don't even know where it is now. I wanted the M.V.P. plaque that I thought I deserved. And in my opinion Barry should be the M.V.P. this year."[12]

Receiving 23 out of 24 first-place votes, Bonds beat out teammates Bobby Bonilla, who hit .302 with 18 home runs; Drabek (who won the Cy Young Award that year); and Andy Van Slyke (.284, 17 home runs, 77 RBIs). Bonds sought to express his gratitude to his teammate Bonilla upon receiving the award. "I wish I could split it and give half to Bobby . . . I wish I could share it. To me, he's just as much of the MVP as I am."[13]

For Bonds, 1990 was the season that would propel him to become respected in his own light. Although he led the league only in the category of slugging percentage (.565), he combined speed and power as no other player had before him. Bonds became the first player in major league history to both drive in and score 100 runs and the first to hit more than 30 home runs, hit over .300, and steal over 50 bases. "I'm proud of that, doing something that no one else has done in the history of baseball."[14] He added, "I decided this year was time for me to get the respect I deserved for myself . . . I had to achieve it myself. My father and Warren Sipe the Pirates' conditioning specialist had me believing I could do anything, that I was invincible."[15]

However invincible Bonds might have seemed during the regular season, the postseason exposed him as a mere mortal. In the League Championship Series against Cincinnati, Bonds hit only .167 going 3 for 18, hitting in a single run and failing to hit a single home run. The Pirates lost in six games. It would be the first of many times in October when Barry Bonds would underperform in the postseason, leading sportswriters to label him a "choker" who, like his father, failed to live up to his potential, yet the numbers do not tell the entire story. In the opening game, for example, Bonds' base-stealing threat created a severe distraction for Reds starting pitcher Jose Rijo, forcing him to throw to first base six times. When Rijo finally pitched the ball, batter Sid Bream hit a two-run homer that tied the game and set up a 4–3 victory for the Pirates.[16]

Despite their disappointing performance in the playoffs, the Pirates were now contenders, even frontrunners. In late 1990, many considered Pittsburgh the best team in baseball, and Bonds was now considered their star. After winning the MVP in November, Bonds expressed his desire to stay with the Pirates and keep on winning. "It's a family oriented team. No one has any jealousy. I just hope we can stay together."[17]

The ownership set out right away to sign Leyland to a two-year contract extension in October, promising him that they would do all they could to keep the team intact. Despite their promises, the Pirates were not able to sign their starting first baseman, Sid Bream, their new leadoff hitter, Wally Backman, or their fourth outfielder, R.J. Reynolds, losing all, along with relief pitcher Ted Power, to free agency.[18] In addition, refusing to concede to the contract demands of Bonds, Bonilla, and Drabek, the team took all three to arbitration. The Pirates won against Bonds and Bonilla. Bonds had asked for a salary of $3.3 million per year but had to accept the team's offer of $2.3 million. If the club could not come to terms with Bonilla during spring training, it faced losing him as well because of a team policy forbidding management from negotiating contracts during the regular season. Van Slyke's contract was also due to expire by the end of 1991, and Pittsburgh faced the possibility of losing two of its three greatest stars before the beginning of 1992.[19]

When the Pirates reported to spring training in late February 1991, the goodwill that Bonds expressed upon receiving his MVP award had evaporated. In its place, there was an unusually dark mood hanging over a team that was a defending division champion. Leyland said that he was concerned about the team's future. "You get your scouts to go out and find as many quality players as possible, which we've done," said Leyland. "Then you have to project them into the future and when they get to be good players, you have to pay them to keep them. You have to be realistic about those things because that's how the system works, like it or not."[20] He expressed particular regret over the loss of Sid Bream, whom the team let go not because of a salary dispute but because Bream wanted to have a no-trade clause in his contract. "He was everything we stood for, a guy who was good for the community, a total team guy and a damn good player."[21]

Bonilla was also unsure of the direction in which the Pirates seemed to be moving. "You don't expect problems to arise. . . . I thought, 'Wow, we won the division, they'll just go out and sign the people they have to sign and let's try to recapture it again. It's a beautiful thing we had happen and let's try to do it again.' . . . Unfortunately that didn't happen. With Pittsburgh it's become economic reasons, I believe. From everything written in the papers, they said they couldn't keep people. So here's where we are now."[22]

The tensions and concerns over the team's future erupted into a full-fledged altercation during the first weeks of Pirate training camp in Bradenton, Florida. At the center of the storm was Barry Bonds. The incident began when Bonds shouted at photographers whom he had asked to stop taking his picture. Team public relations director Jim Lachimia then became involved, also eventually getting into a shouting match with Bonds. A few minutes later, Bonds began arguing and exchanging hostile glances with special instructor Bill Virdon during a fly-ball drill. Finally, Leyland had seen enough. In front of rolling television cameras and dozens of spectators, Leyland lashed out at Bonds in a profanity-laced tirade. "One player's not going to run this club," shouted Leyland. "If you don't want to be here, get the hell out of here. Let's get the show over with or go home. If guys don't want to be here, if guys aren't happy with their money, don't take it out on everybody else." Responding to what he felt was an undermining of his authority, Leyland told Bonds, "I'm the manager of this team."[23]

The entire incident lasted only a few minutes, yet because it was such a public event, it made a tremendous impact upon fans' perceptions of the Pirates and of Bonds. According to Leyland, the shouting match was really indicative of the more general atmosphere that surrounded the team that spring. "There's been a certain amount of tension felt in this camp since we got here. . . . It was probably a matter of time until the tension got broken and, hopefully, that's the end of it."[24] After the argument, Leyland criticized Pirates management as much as he criticized Bonds, saying, "I don't think there's anything worse than an organization that is unsettled. I understand you can't give 21 players multiyear contracts. . . . [But] you can't just look the other way and think that the problems are going to go away."[25]

However, perhaps no event in Bonds' career more cemented his image of a temperamental, sulking, selfish player in the public mind. Bonds' reaction to this event and the way it was covered cemented his feelings that sportswriters were untrustworthy and treacherous. The day after the public confrontation between Bonds and Leyland, *Pittsburgh Post-Gazette* sportswriter Bob Hertzel called Bonds the National League's "Most Volatile Player."[26] Later that month, *Denver Post* columnist Woody Paige coined the nickname Barry "Junk" Bonds, calling Bonds a "Childish Boor" and an "arrogant youngster" whose "antics" had to be put down by Leyland, a "journeyman blue-collar" manager. Paige wrote, "Nobody living in The Real World can sympathize with Bonds, who has spent the spring in Florida pouting because he's playing baseball for only $2,300,000."[27]

Bonds responded that he felt he had been given an unfair shake by sports reporters, whom he saw as looking for negative things to say about him. "I'm tired of always being criticized," he told Hertzel. "I'm always being put down by the media. It doesn't matter what I say, how I say it. They're still going to cut out what they want to cut out and write what they want to write." Bonds contended that it was not accurate for sportswriters to portray him as greedy. It was not the money per se but the amount of respect and recognition that the money conveyed that was important. "If I'm making $2.3 million for the rest of my career, I'm not going to complain. I'm content. . . . All I'm asking is that the Most Valuable Player be paid the way the Most Valuable Player should be paid. . . . I could have come in at $4 million and taken a gamble. But I didn't. I only came in at what I deserve and what I worked for." For Bonds, losing arbitration for a second year was like being "slapped in the face."[28]

While Paige may be right that few would feel much sympathy for Bonds on this point, sports reporters did not often provide a full context for the argument that he had with Leyland. Sportswriters like Paige framed this incident entirely as one surrounding Bonds' unhappiness with his own contract salary. This issue may have been important, if not central, but there may have been much more involved as well. Nevertheless, many interpreted this event as a showdown between a spoiled player and a no-nonsense manager. Detroit Tigers manager Sparky Anderson was among the most vocal in support for Leyland, saying that more managers needed to assert their authority in similar ways. Fans both of Pittsburgh and of opposing teams rallied to the support of Leyland during spring training, booing Bonds at every turn.

As much as newspapers and sports reporters emphasized antagonism between player and manager, however, Bonds and Leyland expressed nothing but support for one another throughout the rest of the spring. The day after the argument, Bonds told Claire Smith of the *New York Times*, "I will never let Jim Leyland down, for nothing in the world. . . . That man has been too good to me. He's treated me with the greatest respect. We've never had a major problem. We never even had a shouting match until now. And it really wasn't a shouting match, but just a big misunderstanding."[29] By the middle of March, Leyland called on spring training crowds to stop booing Bonds. "Maybe I'm sticking my nose in someone else's business but fair is fair," said Leyland. "I think it's gone on long enough and I don't see anything positive coming out of booing Barry Bonds."[30] Directly contradicting Woody Paige's assertion that Bonds "loafed" upon arriving in training camp, Leyland said, "If I was a fan I might boo a player who loafs, but I would never have the right to boo someone like Barry Bonds. He plays hard all the time."[31] Leyland saw Bonds as a player who deserved fans' praise specifically for his work ethic. "Barry Bonds has played as hard this spring as anybody has in any camp. . . . I think when fans pay their money to see a game, they pay to see a guy play hard and he's done that."[32]

Despite predictions that off-field tensions would erode the Pirates winning habits, Pittsburgh and Barry Bonds performed well in 1991.[33] Individually, Bonds had the second best year of his career, hitting .292 with 25 home runs and stealing 43 bases. His 116 runs batted in were the most during any single season of his career to that point, and his 73 strikeouts were the fewest. For his efforts, he finished second in that year's MVP voting and helped to lead the Pirates back as National League Eastern Division Champions. With Bonds, Bonilla, and Van Slyke back in the outfield and with Drabek anchoring the starting rotation, Pittsburgh actually improved upon its record from the previous year, finishing with 98 wins and 64 losses.

Hopes were high in October that the Pirates would finally make a trip back to the World Series. They faced the Atlanta Braves in the National League Championship Series, a team that had gone from being the worst in the league to Division Champion in one year. Led by a strong, young pitching staff that included John Smoltz, Tom Glavine, and Steve Avery, the Braves proved to be a superb match for the Pirates batting order, one that finished first in hitting in the National League.

The Series began on a promising note for the Pirates with a 5–1 victory, yet in the final six games of the Series, Pittsburgh was shut out three times, hitting only .224 as a team during the entire playoffs. Perhaps most frustrating to the team, they returned home from Atlanta before Game 6 with a 3-game-to-2 advantage and failed to score a run in Three Rivers Stadium in their last two games. After the third inning of Game 1, Van Slyke, Bonilla, and Bonds went 0 for 16 with runners in scoring position and 1 for 35 with runners on base. *Pittsburgh Post Gazette* writer Gene Collier called them the "Boys of Bummer." He particularly singled out Bonds for blame, saying that he provided a noticeable lack of leadership to the team. Collier argued that the Braves Terry Pendleton set a selfless, positive example to his teammates, not only playing hard but accepting personal responsibility for a poor hitting performance in the playoffs. "Contrast that to Barry Bonds' litany of excuses (the pitchers, the defense, the time of day, the media)," wrote Collier, "and you start to perhaps see this missing element."[34]

In the off-season, Bonds' fears about losing Bonilla as a teammate came true as the star outfielder signed with the New York Mets. Bonilla, however, ended up hitting only .249 in 1992. Bonds and the Pirates, however, continued to win, finishing the season with a record of 96 wins and 66 losses. Bonds led the Pirates with a .311 batting average, 34 home runs, 103 runs batted in, a .624 slugging percentage, and 39 stolen bases. His performance earned him his second Most Valuable Player award in three years. Once again, the Pirates were champions of the National League's Eastern Division and once again looked to face the Atlanta Braves in the League Championship Series.

This third try for the Pirates was perhaps their most dramatic. The Series would begin and end in Atlanta, giving the Braves home-field advantage, and they would use it as best they could early in the Series, winning the first two games by scores of 5 to 1 and 13 to 5. Once again, Bonds struggled at the plate. During the early part of the Series, he went through a stretch of 28 at-bats with runners on base without a hit.

After returning to Pittsburgh, the Pirates were able to get a complete game performance out of starter Tim Wakefield and won Game 3 by the score of 3 to 2. In Game 4, however, Doug Drabek was not able to hold on for the win, and the Braves triumphed 6 to 4. The Pirates found themselves on the brink of elimination, down 3 games to 1.

In Game 5, however, Pittsburgh responded with a 7-to-1 victory over Braves star Steve Avery and once again got a complete game performance from one of their starters, Bob Walk. As importantly, Bonds seemed to have broken out of his slump, hitting a key RBI double against Avery in his first at-bat. He followed this with a third-inning single, stole second base, and later scored a second run. In addition, he caught a hard-hit line drive off the bat of Ron Gant with one out and former Pirate Sid Bream on second base. "Forget the two hits," said Leyland after the game. "That was the best catch I've ever seen." Before this game, Bonds was hitting .091 in the Series. After the loss in Game 4, he spent 2½ hours talking with Leyland in his office. "It was best friends talking," said Leyland. "It was a positive, emotional conversation. I told Barry to forget the past, to go out and relax." Sun Bonds, Barry's wife, also flew Bonilla up from Florida to surprise his friend. All of this seemed to have an impact, and after Game 5, Bonds and the Pirates flew down to Atlanta with renewed confidence that this would finally be their year.

It did not take long for Bonds to show that confidence once the Series began again in Atlanta. Coming to the plate for the first time in the second inning, Bonds led off with a home run that soared over the right field wall and scoreboard. By the time the inning was over, Bonds, on base again after another hit, was thrown out at the plate while trying to score the Pirates ninth run against Atlanta starter Tom Glavine. It was a stunning explosion for a Pirates team that had become known for their silent bats in the postseason. The eight-run inning was one run short of a playoff record. Despite giving up two home runs to David Justice, Pirates starter Tim Wakefield was able to hold on for a complete game 13–4 victory.[35]

The victory forced a deciding Game 7 to the Series, and Pittsburgh seemed to be in good shape with a rejuvenated line-up and a rested bullpen. Game 7, however, would become a nightmare for the Pirates, one that would focus once again upon Barry Bonds. Once again, the game was a pitchers' dual, this time between ace starters Drabek and Smoltz. Pittsburgh got to Smoltz early, scoring a single run in the first inning, then adding another in the sixth. Drabek, on the other hand, pitched eight nearly flawless innings of shutout ball. He had thrown 120 pitches when he took the mound in the ninth with a 2–0 lead. After three batters, however, the bases were loaded with no outs, and Leyland pulled Drabek for closer Stan Belinda. The Braves Ron Gant was the first to face the reliever, and he hit a rocketing line drive into left field that looked as if it would leave the ballpark and give the Braves a victory. Instead, Bonds was able to chase it down and catch it at the wall. Terry Pendleton, who had led off the inning with a double, tagged from third and scored, making the score 2–1. Damon Berryill then walked, loading the bases again. Brian Hunter came up with a chance to end the game with a hit, but he popped out to shortstop Jose Lind. It looked as if the Pirates might escape with a victory.

It only prolonged the inevitable agony. Francisco Cabrera, who had spent most of the season playing for Richmond in the minor leagues, came to the plate. With the count at 2–1, Cabrera hit a line drive between short and third base. Justice scored easily from third, and Bream took off from second determined to score. With two outs, the sluggish Bream at least was able to run on the pitch, and it gave him a significant head start. Bonds fielded the ball perfectly and came up throwing. The throw was a little high, and Bream slid under the tag, and the Braves had beaten the Pirates for the National League pennant for the second consecutive year.

Sports Illustrated writer Tim Kurkjian aptly called it "the cruelest game." "If Bream had instead been a speedy pinch runner and if Bonds's [*sic*] throw had been just a little bit off, the play at the plate might not have been close. But, no, that wouldn't have been excruciating enough. Bonds's throw was perfect. And Bream is one of the game's slowest men, as well as a former Pirate. He barely—barely—beat the tag of his friend Mike LaValliere." Below Bonds' picture in the story, Kurkjian wrote, "Bonds may very well be the 1992 MVP, but in Atlanta he was a Miserable Vanquished Pirate."[36]

Not all fans or sportswriters were as charitable toward Bonds as Kurkjian, however. Thomas Boswell of the *Washington Post* wrote, "And here Sid came, running faster than he ever had in his life and slower than you could imagine your Uncle Ralph on Sunday afternoon. Where was Barry? Playing on the warning track? Well, almost. Bonds played a conspicuously deep left field the entire inning. But he came charging, scooping and, finally, unleashing as strong a heave as you'll see to the plate. If it had been on line, Sid Bream would have been back out at first base with a glove in the 10th inning and they'd be measuring third base coach Jimy Williams for a coffin in a shallow grave in the morning. If the throw had only been a little off line—a pretty good throw—you can bet umpire Randy Marsh would have called him out on general principles. If you're

Sid Bream, you've got to score clean to get any calls. But Bonds's throw was at least two paces up the first base line. Spanky LaValliere did all a catcher can do. Which means Bream was safe by six inches."[37]

While Boswell implicitly stated that Bonds was at fault for Bream's miraculous score from second, many Pirates fans explicitly blamed him once again for failing to lead their team into the World Series. When Bonds returned to play against the Pirates as a San Francisco Giant nearly ten years later, he was booed, not only as a member of the opposing team but as a player who had what *Pittsburgh Post-Gazette* writer Bob Smizik called a "bittersweet bond" with the fans. As Smizik writes, "what seems to gall people is that Bonds couldn't throw out Bream on a dash to home that remains one of the saddest moments in Pittsburgh sports history." Smizik goes on to admit, however, "Truth be known, not many men could have thrown out Bream. What is forgotten is that there were two outs, so Bream was running as the ball was hit. Bonds had to come in and over to make the play. When he threw his momentum was carrying him away from home and he was throwing against his body."[38]

Bonds' salary that year was $4,800,000, but his contract was coming to a close, and it looked almost certain that the Pirates could no longer afford his paycheck. Following the loss to Atlanta, Barry Bonds went on the free agent market, and rumors circulated among sports reporters about where he would end up: with the Yankees, the Mets, the Dodgers, and even the Braves. The Pirates, meanwhile, were about to lose their key starter, Doug Drabek, along with Bonds. For Pittsburgh, that October night in Atlanta, one out away from the World Series, would be the closest they would come to the World Series in more than a decade. For Bonds, it would be a bittersweet final moment playing under Jim Leyland, a manager whom he had grown to admire and respect as profoundly as any. In December, Bonds signed with the San Francisco Giants for a contract that guaranteed him $43.75 million over six years and included incentives and deferred payments that added up to $60 million. Bonds was returning home, and he was doing so as the highest-paid player in baseball history.

NOTES

1. "Stat of the Day," *Washington Post*, June 5, 1986.
2. Jim Donaghy, "Sports News," Associated Press, April 13, 1990.
3. Alan Robinson, "An AP Sport Scene," Associated Press, July 25, 1989.
4. David Steele, phone interview with author, February 27, 2002.
5. Travers, *Barry Bonds*, 51.
6. "Pirates Make Investment in Bonds," Associated Press, July 31, 1988.

7. Ibid.

8. William Ladson, "The Complete Player," *Sporting News*, July 12, 1999, 12.

9. "Pirates Sharing the Wealth," *Bergen Record*, November 20, 1990, D5.

10. Robinson, "An AP Sport Scene."

11. Donaghy, "Sports News."

12. Dave Anderson, "Sports of the Times," *New York Times*, October 5, 1990, 29A.

13. "Pirates Sharing the Wealth," *Bergen Record*.

14. Claire Smith, "Bonds Is Voted MVP in Landslide," *New York Times*, November 20, 1990, 13B.

15. "Pirates Sharing the Wealth," *Bergen Record*.

16. Anderson, "Sports of the Times," 29A.

17. "Pirates Sharing the Wealth," *Bergen Record*.

18. Bob Hertzel, "Pirates Show Strain from Tension Spring," *Pittsburgh Post-Gazette*, March 5, 1991.

19. Ibid.; Russell Schneider, "Bonds Fight, Player Losses May Hurt Pirates," *Cleveland Plain Dealer*, March 19, 1991; Marc Topkin, "Keeping Pirates Shipshape," *St. Petersburg Times*, March 23, 1991, 5C.

20. Schneider, "Bonds Fight, Player Losses May Hurt Pirates."

21. Ibid.

22. Topkin, "Keeping Pirates Shipshape," 5C.

23. "Leyland, Bonds Dispute," *New York Times*, March 5, 1991, B12.

24. Hertzel, "Pirates Show Strain from Tension Spring."

25. Ibid.

26. Bob Hertzel, "Bonds Blames Bad-Guy Label on the Media," *Pittsburgh Post-Gazette*, March 5, 1991, C1.

27. Woody Paige, "FAM-I-LEE IN TURMOIL: Barry Bonds Never Wanted to Be Problem," *Denver Post*, March 18, 1991, 1D.

28. Hertzel, "Bonds Blames Bad-Guy Label on the Media," C1.

29. Claire Smith, "Bonds Says He's Puzzled by Bad-Guy Image," *New York Times*, March 6, 1991, 23D.

30. "Leyland Says Boos to Bonds Are Undeserved," *(Ft. Lauderdale) Sun-Sentinel*, March 18, 1991, 5C.

31. Jerome Holtzman, "Economy Plan Cuts into Pirates Lineup," *Chicago Tribune*, March 26, 1991, 7.

32. "Leyland Says Boos to Bonds Are Undeserved."

33. Schneider, "Bonds Fight, Player Losses May Hurt Pirates."

34. Gene Collier, "For Want of a Leader, Series Was Lost," *Pittsburgh Post-Gazette*, October 18, 1991, D1.

35. Terence Moore, "Avalanche Second Did Wonders for Bucs," *Atlanta Journal and Constitution*, October 14, 1992, D4; Rod Beaton, "Pirates Shell-Shock Braves 13-4//Wakefield, 13-hit Attack Forces NL Series Game 7," *USA Today*, October 14, 1992, 1C.

36. Tim Kurkjian, "The Cruelest Game," *Sports Illustrated* 77, no. 18, October 26, 1992.

37. Thomas Boswell, "Cabrera's Lightning Stroke Anoints Braves," *Washington Post*, October 15, 1992, D1.

38. Bob Smizik, "Fans Have Bittersweet Bond with Barry," *Pittsburgh Post-Gazette*, August 5, 2002, C3.

SALVAGING A FRANCHISE,
1993

After weeks of rumors, negotiations, and drama, Barry Bonds signed a contract with the San Francisco Giants worth roughly $43.75 million over six years. Among the features in the salary structure, Bonds earned a $2.5 million signing bonus, as well as bonuses for winning Most Valuable Player. The contract guaranteed that he would earn annual salaries that would start at $4 million in 1993 and end at $8.5 million in 1998. *San Francisco Chronicle* baseball writer Tim Keown calculated that Bonds (based upon previous performances) would earn $49,603 per hit, $214,460 per home run, $70,792.88 per run batted in, and $52,083.36 per game.[1]

At the end of the 1993 season, *USA Today*'s sports section printed their list of "Baseball's All-Overpaid Team," which actually listed players whom they considered either overpaid or undervalued based upon their contracts and their performances. At $4,219,175, Bonds was named an honorary member of the All-*Underpaid* team.[2] It was that kind of season for Barry Bonds.

There are, of course, the statistics—a .336 batting average (fourth in the league); and league-leading numbers in slugging percentage (.677, the highest to that date in franchise history), on-base percentage (.458), total bases (365), runs batted in (123), and home runs (46). One can even cite his third Most Valuable Player award in four seasons, his Associated Press Major League Player of the Year award, his consensus All-Star ranking, and his fourth consecutive Gold Glove Award. None of his numbers or awards, however, adequately express the magnitude of Bonds' performance in 1993. If Bonds had not so completely obliterated any imaginable expectation of what a baseball player could do over the next decade, 1993 might have been considered the season of a lifetime for Bonds—or for any player for that matter.

When Bonds signed with the Giants, he made the choice to leave a team that was one out away from the World Series to join a team that was literally on life support. After winning the National League West pennant in 1987 and the National League title in 1989, the Giants had gone into a tailspin at the beginning of the new decade. They finished fourth in 1991 with a 75–87 record and fifth in 1992, losing an embarrassing 90 games. Owner Bob Lurie, unable to persuade any municipalities in the Bay Area to use public funds to build a new baseball stadium for his team, had decided to sell the Giants. It looked as if the team might move to New Orleans when Peter McGowan, chairman and chief executive officer of Safeway supermarkets, made a bid to buy the team and keep it in San Francisco.

In fact, not only was Bonds choosing to sign with a team that seemed to have an uncertain future, but it was uncertain at that time whether he would even end up with the Giants even after his name was on the contract. When Bonds signed with the Giants, the owners of the other teams in Major League Baseball had not even approved McGowan's bid. If they had denied McGowan, Bonds would have ended up back on the free agent market the next week.

McGowan, however, did end up getting his bid approved, and he strove to give his new team a new look. He hired Dusty Baker to manage his Giants and hoped that the addition of Bonds would create a stronger line-up that could take pressure off the Giants only other bona fide superstars, Will Clark and Matt Williams.

Unfortunately, Clark was not able to perform up to the levels he had previously in his career, hitting .283 with only 14 home runs in 1993. It really did not matter. Bonds carried the team on his back to a record of 103 wins and 59 losses. It was the second best record in the National League that year, but unfortunately for the Giants, it was also the second best record in their division. Nevertheless, Barry Bonds had led the Giants to one of the most stunning turnarounds in baseball history and turned San Francisco into a baseball team that would be a consistent contender for the next decade.

When Barry Bonds signed with the Giants, he was not only choosing a new team but returning to his roots. Once more, Giants fans would see the familiar name of Bonds on the back of a Giants uniform. The Giants even hired Barry's father as a batting coach for the team, and Bonds was returning to play under a manager whom he had known literally since the day he was born, Dusty Baker.

Josh Suchon, who covers the Giants for the *Oakland Tribune* and who wrote a book about the season in which Bonds broke the single-season home-run record, points out that the Bonds and Baker families were very close to one another when Bobby and Dusty were growing up during the 1950s and early 1960s in Riverside, California. "Dusty Baker's dad was Bobby Bonds' little league coach," says Suchon, "and Bobby Bonds' mom babysat Dusty. So it would be very frequent that Dusty's dad would pick up Bobby to go to little league practice, and drop off his son Dusty at his house so Dusty would be babysat as he went to their house." A few years younger than Bobby Bonds, Baker grew up idolizing his babysitter's son. According to Suchon, "[Baker] played four sports—baseball, basketball, football, and track—because Bobby played four sports. He played linebacker because Bobby was a linebacker. He did the long jump because Bobby did the long jump. Everything that he did . . . athletically was because of what Bobby did." Suchon even points out, "The day that Bobby Bonds had his first son Barry, Dusty went to the hospital with his dad and held Barry in his arms. . . . For two families to be that close and then thirty years later to end up having Dusty manage Barry, to me . . . it's just amazing."[3]

Surrounded by familiar faces and playing only a few miles from where he grew up, Bonds thrived as a Giant, yet if 1993 was the year in which the Bonds would truly become recognized as a franchise player, it was also the year that he would become a target of media criticism to match his offensive production statistics. Bonds' hot season, and the Giants remarkable start, put the spotlight on him as never before.

Bonds' first at-bat for the Giants on their home opener was a home run. As Giants beat writer Bruce Jenkins described it in the *San Francisco Chronicle*, "Barry Bonds stepped up in the second inning, first home at bat in the season, and basically said, 'Here's the $43 million, here's the attitude, here's the reason I'm here.' In a wonderfully fearless display, he jacked a long, hooking drive into the right-field seats, a first impression for the ages."[4] By end of April, it was clear that the Giants and Bonds were having a special season, and by the beginning of June, the team had a record of 33 wins and 18 losses. The *Washington Post's* Thomas Boswell put Bonds' performance at the top of his list of surprises for the early part of the season. "He's going to win the Triple Crown this year. Nobody's done it since 1967. But the stars are aligned. You need a guy the whole league holds in awe. That's Bonds. To other players and stat freaks, he's been in the Mickey Mantle or Willie Mays class for three years. 'I told my father it's like Little League for him,' Giants shortstop Royce Clayton said of Bonds. 'He goes two for four and gets ticked off.' Bonds has gotten off to a suitably ridiculous start—on a pace for 157 RBIs, 43 homers and a .421 average. In the batting race, his weakest area, only one player is within 65 points of him. That's the head start he needs. At 28, he's at his peak. Who says nobody's worth $43 million?"[5]

Bonds did not win the Triple Crown. The numbers he put up in 1993, however, were good enough to have earned him that title during five of the previous seven seasons.[6] More importantly, his performance was almost good enough to have sent his team to the National League Championship Series. The Giants 103 wins in 1993 make them one of the best teams in baseball history to have failed to play in the postseason.

It was, indeed, a remarkable season. The Giants led the Atlanta Braves in the race for the National League West pennant for most of the summer, despite the fact that the Braves had signed another ace, Greg Maddux, to their starting rotation. Atlanta, however, turned around after acquiring Fred McGriff following the All-Star break. By the end of August, the Braves had swept the Giants in a crucial three-game series in San Francisco. In September, the Giants went into a free fall, losing 8 consecutive games, and 9 out of 10 between the 5th and the 15th. It looked as if the Giants had returned to their old form.

They responded, however, and rebounded back into the race, winning their next 4 games and 14 out of their next 16. The Giants and Braves went into the last game of the season locked in a tie. Knowing that the Braves had already won their final game at home, the Giants took the field against the Dodgers in Los Angeles and were completely dominated, losing by a score of 12–1. Once again, October would prove to be the cruelest month for Barry Bonds.

Perhaps even crueler than the month of October was the corps of reporters who covered Bonds during the season. His MVP performance in 1992 with the Pirates and his monumental contract had made Bonds a target of media scrutiny. Since being called up by the Pirates, Bonds had long had an uncomfortable relationship with the press. Reporters alleged that Bonds treated them rudely, did not show up for interviews, and had a cold relationship with his teammates. By 1993, their criticisms became louder, to the point that they almost overshadowed Bonds' performance on the field.

One of the first salvos in the media attack came from sportswriter and bestselling author John Feinstein in his book *Play Ball*, a reflection on the 1992 major league season. The inside flap of the dust jacket for the book announced that Feinstein provides "revealing glimpses" of such "newer stars" as "Bobby Bonds." Things only got worse for Barry inside the book.

After praising Jim Leyland's managing, Feinstein quotes Bonds as saying about his former manager, "We all know we can count on anything he says. He's just not capable of dealing with people any way but straight ahead." Feinstein goes on to write, "The same could not be said of Bonds. There was no better all around player in the National League. At twenty-eight, he was on his way to a second MVP in three years and a multimillion-dollar contract with someone, since he would be the number-one free agent in the fall. He was handsome and articulate, the son of Bobby Bonds, a great major league player himself, and capable of being as charming as anyone in the game when the mood struck him. . . . The mood didn't strike him often. He could be rude, not only to outsiders, but to his teammates. They accepted him because he played hard and worked hard every day, but they were as mystified by him as everyone else was." In the passage on Bonds, Feinstein quotes Pirates vice president of public relations Rick Cerrone as saying about him, "You have to remember one thing at all times when you're dealing with Barry. . . . This is not an adult. This is a nine-year-old. He's a nine-year-old kid in the body of an extraordinary twenty-eight-year-old athlete. He's not a horrible guy, he's just a very immature person." Feinstein goes on to argue that a recent softening of Bonds' image was only the result of coaching from his recently hired agent, Dennis Gilbert.[7]

In May, *Sports Illustrated* profiled Bonds in a major feature article. The headline read, "The Importance of Being Barry." Author Richard Hoffer describes Bonds as selfish, rude, and self-centered. Hoffer had arrived in San Francisco to do a story on Bonds' return to the Bay Area, and Bonds had repeatedly rescheduled and canceled interview dates with the reporter, angry about his previous treatment by the magazine.

Hoffer, in turn, reacted against the way that Bonds had repeatedly snubbed him with a devastatingly bitter article in which he describes Bonds comparing paychecks with teammates, bragging about money and accomplishments, and generally exhibiting the maturity of a teenager. Hoffer wrote, "Once this spring, or so the story goes, Bonds hit an impressive home run, then turned in the batting cage to face his teammates and said, 'Am I not a special—person, or what?' Bonds claims it wasn't that way at all. He says he made a boastful comment, but that it was meant to be playful and not to be mistaken for arrogance. When Bonds is arrogant, there is no mistaking it."

There is also no mistaking that Hoffer did not agree with Bonds' interpretation of this incident. In the article, he provides an extremely unflattering biography of Bonds, noting that it is not Bonds' strutting around the base paths after hitting a home run that makes people see him as a unlikable personality. Nor is it an attitude that many find arrogant. Rather, Hoffer writes that it is Bonds' "complaining, his rudeness, his insensitivity to teammates [that] can wear a franchise out."

Hoffer paints a picture of Bonds as a deeply narcissistic person, whose self-centered nature was in evidence even during his high school sports career. There, according to Hoffer, Bonds held his classmates at arm's length but cherished the attention of coaches. He had the same attitude in college, writes Hoffer, where teammates, described by his coach Barry Brock as "half white with a redneck factor," turned a cold shoulder to their flashy new teammate. When Bonds returned to the Pirates clubhouse for the first time as a Giant, his former teammates exhibited this same reaction. Hoffer writes that they hardly looked up from their card games. Hoffer criticizes Bonds for lashing out at his teammate Jeff King while a Pirate for not playing with a severe back injury during the 1990 playoffs or claiming that racism motivated the front office to let Bobby Bonilla go to the Mets. According to Hoffer, almost nobody likes Bonds except for an inner circle of friends and former coaches. Hoffer wrote that the Pittsburgh media grew to despise Bonds. Even though he gave them an occasional good quote, they were happy to say good-bye to their rude and moody star.[8]

Not all sportswriters were as vitriolic as Hoffer, but his piece in *Sports Illustrated* did seem to represent one part of a larger pattern of media scrutiny directed toward Bonds' psyche. Thomas Boswell, a month after praising Bonds' astounding performance that spring, joined the bandwagon of reporters conducting armchair psychology on Barry Bonds. In a relatively sympathetic column in June, Boswell explored the paradox that Bonds' personality seemed to pose for reporters. "Barry Bonds is a chip off the old block, all right. Unfortunately, the chip is on his shoulder, just like it was on his dad's. If a father gets that chip knocked on the floor often enough—if he gets traded enough and bad-mouthed enough and goes as much as five years at a time without getting a job anywhere in the game—isn't it possible that the oldest son might pick up that chip and wear it like a family badge of honor?" Boswell goes on to describe Bonds and his teammates watching the National Basketball Association Conference Final on television finals while in a locker room after a game.

> There's only one TV and Barry Bonds has his chair in the front row. Lots of players make comments. But Bonds makes the most and the loudest. He doesn't really have a social knack. His comments don't quite blend. But then neither does he. Nobody in the room is dressed like Bonds. He looks like a hip Hollywood fashion show. Nobody else has a sweater covered with colorful geometric shapes and a new style of collar that looks a bit like a Nehru jacket. Nobody else wears their gold jewelry outside their collar. Nobody else has mustard-colored silk socks with little black animals stitched on them. Or shoes that look a bit like slippers. His shoes are, well, what the heck are they? They're the next cool thing, the cutting edge, the place where Bonds wants to be before everybody else, even if they might resent it.[9]

San Francisco Chronicle columnist Lowell Cohn wrote in May 1993 of Bonds' difficult relationship with the media, only in a way that expressed a sense of admiration. Cohn compares Bonds to Michael Jordan, noting that the latter loves the media spotlight, endorses as many commercial products as he can, and always seems to want to be the center of attention. Bonds, in contrast, "disdains fame. He said that he feels uncomfortable that his shoe company wants to put up a Barry Bonds mural in San Francisco. He tries to avoid every interview the Giants ask him to perform. He is cool to the fans in left field, although they already worship him." Cohn concludes, however, that Bonds' discomfort with fame actually makes him seem more human "and more likable."[10]

For sportswriters around the country, the Bonds persona had risen to the level of metaphor. For example, when Steve Aschburner of the *Minneapolis Star and Tribune* did a profile of Chicago White Sox slugger Frank Thomas, he referred to him as "Barry Bonds pumped up, minus the speed, the defense, the dangling cross and the attitude."[11]

Who among these sportswriters are right or wrong about Barry Bonds is hard to say for anyone who does not know him personally. Whether Bonds is rude, arrogant, mean, or a jerk is, in many respects, beside the point. If Bonds does treat sportswriters in the way that many have described, then it is no surprise that so many began to describe him in unflattering terms. It is more of a question as to why this particular image has become the dominant one for Barry Bonds, so much so that during some of the greatest moments of his playing career, he has received some of his most negative publicity. However if, as Hoffer describes, most baseball players are selfish, arrogant, and immature, it deserves questioning as to why this image has become so clearly focused on Bonds and not on other players. Perhaps no other player has declared more his desire for the media to focus only upon his playing abilities. Yet, ironically, over the next years as a Giant, Bonds' personality would become as much a part of his career as his exploits on the playing field. The events of the coming year would not help Bonds' image nor that of any other highly paid baseball player and would cast a pall over baseball for much of the next decade.

NOTES

1. Tim Keown, "Bonds Is Coming, Stewart Is Going," *San Francisco Chronicle*, December 9, 1992.

2. "Baseball's All-Overpaid Team," *USA Today*, October 29, 1993, 3C.

3. Josh Suchon, phone interview with author, May 15, 2003.

4. Bruce Jenkins, "Dream Day," *San Francisco Chronicle*, April 13, 1993, E1.

5. Thomas Boswell, "Spin on the Season's First Month," *Washington Post*, May 9, 1993, D11.

6. Travers, *Barry Bonds: Baseball's Superman*, 72.

7. John Feinstein, *Play Ball: The Life and Troubled Times of Major League Baseball* (New York: Villard Books, 1993), 287.

8. Richard Hoffer, "The Importance of Being Barry," *Sports Illustrated*, May 24, 1993, 12.

9. Thomas Boswell, "Barry Bonds Has an Abrasive Personality, Penchant for Conflict," *Washington Post*, June 6, 1993, D1.

10. Lowell Cohn, "Dominant Force," *San Francisco Chronicle*, May 7, 1993, E1.

11. Steve Aschburner, "So Good It Hurts," *Minneapolis Star and Tribune*, August 29, 1993, 14C.

4

A Tarnished Image for Bonds and Baseball, 1994

"Baseball," wrote the *Washington Post*'s Michael Wilbon, "can go to hell."[1] Nobody could sum up the sentiments of baseball fans—or perhaps it would be more accurate to say former baseball fans—better after the summer of 1994. After months of negotiations, the owners of Major League Baseball franchises and the Major League Players Association failed to reach an agreement by a self-imposed deadline, and on August 12 they stopped playing what might have been one of their most memorable seasons ever. Tony Gwynn of the San Diego Padres had a realistic opportunity to become the first major league player since Ted Williams in 1941 finished the season with an average of over .400; Matt Williams of the Giants was on pace to break the single-season home-run record of 61 set over thirty-two years earlier by Roger Maris in 1961; the lowly Montreal Expos looked to be headed toward the playoffs; and the Cleveland Indians were destined to win their first birth in the postseason in forty years. Instead, stadiums were empty in late August and September. The first year of playoffs under baseball's realigned division structure never took place, and the World Series, which had been played through two world wars, a depression, and even an earthquake, was canceled for the first time since 1904.

Baseball fans were outraged. They had paid for publicly funded major league ballparks with their taxes and had seen the average price of tickets and ballpark concessions skyrocket over the previous two years. To most, the work stoppage seemed like little more than a petty squabble among spoiled millionaires, one that, like most others of this sort, gets resolved to their mutual advantage while leaving the average citizen empty-handed. Highly paid players most often bore the brunt of fan resentment, and no player was more highly paid, and more often bore the brunt, than Barry Bonds.

Bonds was well on the way to having another outstanding season when the games were suspended. In 112 games played, Bonds hit 37 home runs and had a realistic chance at hitting 50 for the season. With a .312 batting average, 81 runs batted in, 29 stolen bases, and one of the highest fielding percentages of his career, Bonds might have called 1994 a successful year on the field.

Fans and sportswriters paid little attention to on-field accomplishments in 1994, however, because by the end of the summer, there was nothing happening on the field. In the case of Barry Bonds, his more unsuccessful life off the field became the source of public attention. In June 1994, Bonds had filed for legal separation from his wife of six years, Sun. The previous August, Barry and Sun were involved in a physical altercation in which police had been called to their home. Ultimately, the San Mateo County district attorney's office did not file charges against Barry, citing a lack of evidence and cooperation from Sun. However, the details of the fight were widely reported in the local and national media. According to the Atherton, California, police report filed the night of the incident, Sun told authorities that she and Barry had become involved in an argument over the housekeeper while on the way home from a Giants game. The argument escalated, according to Sun, to the point where Barry grabbed her and threw her against a car and later grabbed her around the neck and partially threw her down a set of stairs.[2]

The event actually passed with little attention when it happened, yet over the next year, it gained a strange significance as it resonated with the murder of Nicole Browne Simpson and Ronald Goldman the following June. Simpson, as most remember, had been married to football star O. J. Simpson. After a long, slow speed chase through the freeways of Los Angeles, O. J. Simpson had been arrested as the primary suspect in the brutal murder. During the summer of 1994, the Simpson murder case was on its way to becoming one of the most publicized and racially divisive murder trials of the late twentieth century.

After Simpson's arrest, television news programs, supermarket tabloids, and mainstream newspapers all began broadcasting and publishing details of his life with Nicole. News outlets replayed police tape recordings of Nicole screaming into the phone to report a violent outburst by her husband, who could be heard yelling and pounding on a door in the background. Whatever differences there might have been between the Bonds incident and the marriage of O. J. and Nicole Brown Simpson, the O. J. Simpson case had become a filter through which many other famous celebrities and athletes would be viewed. In particular, it provided a story and a set of images that resonated with widely circulated judgments and ideas regarding African American male athletes, ones that have been part of the way black athletes have been represented for more than a century.

The first black athletes to rise to national celebrity status were jockeys and boxers in the late nineteenth and early twentieth centuries. This was a time period in which popular white fears of black men were escalating. The imposition of Jim Crow laws mandating separate facilities for whites and blacks during the late nineteenth century, for example, was, in part, predicated upon a view of independent black male behavior as sexually uncontrolled, focused upon immediate gratification, and unpredictably violent. Popular representations of African American men in films such as *The Birth of a Nation* (1915) reinforced these images for millions of viewers, even helping to spark a revival of the Ku Klux Klan. In 1910, a powerfully built, self-confident, and flamboyant African American man named Jack Johnson won, and later defended, the heavyweight boxing world championship. Many whites reacted with fear and horror, organizing mobs that invaded and rioted through the streets of predominantly black neighborhoods and apartment buildings. Before Johnson's first title defense, "Gentleman" Jim Corbett confidently predicted that Johnson would lose due to what Corbett thought was the black race's fear and awe of whites. Ironically, it was a white population, unable to accept black equality in American society that feared and vilified a black champion, who not only displayed talents as a fighter but also openly dated white women.

The Jack Johnson story and its historical legacy are part of what made Simpson's case meaningful, and, in turn, these became what made the Bonds divorce meaningful as well. In November 1994, Bonds' marital problems became linked to Simpson in a paternity suit that pornographic film actress Jennifer Peace filed against him in Los Angeles Superior Court. Peace not only had accused Bonds of fathering her child but had been, according the Associated Press, "linked" to Al Cowlings, the former University of Southern California football player who drove O. J. Simpson on his famous chase through Southern California. This obscure link, an unproven accusation, was enough to have made this story appear in the *Washington Post* and *USA Today*.

In addition, Bonds' marital troubles became increasingly framed within a wider set of events and emotions surrounding the baseball work stoppage. Shortly after play was suspended, Bonds went before San Mateo County Superior Court judge George Taylor to ask that his child support payments be cut in half due to Bonds' loss of income during the strike. The Associated Press reported that Taylor granted Bonds his wish and after the hearing asked the star for his autograph. Reporters jumped on this story as a prime example of the greed, insensitivity, and selfishness of baseball players. Gene Seymour of the *(Springfield, IL) Journal-Register* gave Bonds a "Golden Turkey" award just before Thanksgiving for his request, and Associated Press writer Hal Bock wrote about it at the end of the year as an event symbolic of the corruption indicative of professional athletics.[3] "Never in sports has greed been so obvious, so conspicuous from all sides," wrote Bock. He added, with a note of sarcasm, "Bonds, after all, in the second year of a six-year, $43.75 million contract, was on strike and not getting a paycheck. The sympathetic commissioner reduced the payments, then asked the outfielder for his autograph. Later, in an apparent attack of common sense, Taylor reversed his ruling. It was not immediately clear, however, whether he returned the autograph."

As Bonds' divorce proceedings began over the next year, its details continued to plague the star's public image. In March 1995, while the baseball strike was grinding on, Bonds entered divorce hearings in San Mateo County Court. Attorneys for Sun Bonds argued that Barry Bonds coerced his future wife into signing an unfair prenuptial agreement that should be disallowed. The agreement stipulated that Sun Bonds was not entitled to any property or income that Barry earned during their marriage. Had it not been for the agreement, Sun would have been automatically entitled to half of Barry's earnings and property. Sun Bonds' attorneys recalled that she was at a severe disadvantage when she signed the agreement.[4]

The couple met when Sun was working as a bartender in Montreal in 1987 and married shortly thereafter in 1988 at a wedding in Las Vegas. At the time, Barry Bonds was making just over $100,000 a year playing for the Pittsburgh Pirates. A Swedish immigrant, Sun was still having trouble speaking and understanding English. Nevertheless, Barry Bonds, with his lawyers present, had his fiancée sign the prenuptial agreement. Sun did not have a lawyer present at the time that she signed the agreement.

Ultimately, Judge Judith Kozloski ruled in favor of Barry Bonds, saying that "at the time of the signing, the terms of the agreement were fair." She continued that "for several years [Sun Bonds] lived an opulent lifestyle and enjoyed many advantages that she would not have had if she had not been [Barry Bonds'] wife" and concluded that with the $30,000 a month that she would get in alimony and child support, Sun would be living a life "far above that which she knew before marriage." Details of the Bonds marriage became uglier during hearings to determine permanent spousal support later in December 1995. Sun Bonds testified that Barry had kicked her while she was pregnant during their marriage, angered over her desire to start a career as a cosmetologist. In April 1999, the California State First District appeals court overturned Kozloski's ruling by a 2–1 vote, a ruling that Barry Bonds appealed to the state Supreme Court, which reversed once more, upholding the Bonds prenuptial agreement.[5]

Regardless of the legal rulings, Bonds' behavior projected an unflattering image of a selfish and greedy professional athlete. The police reports of spousal abuse, the details of his prenuptial agreement, and his request to cut child support payments all suggest that Barry Bonds was responsible for much of the unfavorable press he received during this time period. Nevertheless, fascination with Bonds' personal travails is perhaps more significant because it seemed to confirm a story about him that sportswriters and baseball fans already thought that they knew. His divorce commanded an unusual amount of media attention, even though Bonds is hardly the only baseball player to have been involved in an ugly divorce or even to have asked for leniency from child support payments. Relatively few took notice when millionaire baseball players Tom Candiotti and Candy Maldonado went before Contra Costa (California) County Superior Court to also ask for reductions in their child support payments during the strike.[6] Fewer remembered that Anaheim Angels prospect John Fischel was actually arrested during a spring training game for failing to pay $50,000 in child support.[7]

What is more, other players seemed to have enjoyed an almost heroic public reputation in spite of, or maybe even because of, their disreputable behavior off the field. In 1993, Philadelphia Phillies outfielder Lenny Dykstra was praised by teammates and sportswriters alike for his hustle and strong hitting, earning the nickname "nails," yet he served a year suspension during his career for illegal gambling and missed most of the 1991 season recovering from a severe car accident that took place while he was driving under the influence of alcohol. In 1992, a *Philadelphia Magazine* reporter witnessed Dykstra cursing loudly in an Atlantic City casino while having to be restrained from attacking another casino customer. When sports agent Alan Meersand parted company with Dykstra in 1994, he said about the star center fielder, "I no longer wish to represent a player who curses at women and children. . . . He's everything I don't want my son to grow up to be. He has no respect for anything, including himself."[8]

Regardless of his checkered past, most sportswriters merely referred to Dykstra as a colorful character. When Dykstra expressed doubt in the fall of 1994 as to whether the players' union would stick together in the event of a protracted strike, *Minneapolis Star-Tribune* reporter referred to him as the "sometimes goofy" slugger for the Phillies. Bonds, on the other hand, was never presented in such lovable terms. Whether or not he was actually any more self-centered than any other Major League Baseball player, the image that Bonds projected seemed a perfect lightning rod for fan resentment during the baseball strike. The *Montreal Gazette*, for example, printed an article in early March 1995 noting that Bonds would lose $42,000 per day during the strike. Below a photograph accompanying the article the text read "Barry Bonds. He's a big loser."[9]

As the *Montreal Gazette* article illustrates, a major reason that Bonds became a target of fan anger was his exceptionally high salary. In fact, Bond has been the highest paid player in baseball the previous season. Fans had little sympathy for any players whose average salary was $1.6 million a year, and their criticism grew more intense when the players' union and representatives for team owners could not come to an agreement before the September 14 settlement deadline. This meant the first cancellation of the World Series since 1904, when New York Giants skipper John McGraw refused to play the champion of the American League. Writing for *McLean's*, Bob Levin summed up the sentiments of most fans when he stated, "Money may not be the root of all evil, but it certainly has rotted the core of professional baseball."[10]

Of course, money had always been at the core of professional baseball since its official origins in 1869; otherwise, it would never have been considered "professional" in the first place. The forces leading to the 1994 strike were neither unique to that time period nor the fault of individually greedy players alone. Rather, they had been part of the fabric of the sport since the late nineteenth century, a fabric that embodied tensions between management and players that were strong enough to have created work stoppages in 1972, 1973, 1976, 1980, 1981, 1985, and 1990 even before the famous strike of 1994–1995.

At the root of the conflict between baseball team owners and players is a contract restriction that became a standard component of major league work agreements in 1880 known as the reserve clause. This short proviso stated that players were bound to a specific team with whom they originally signed a contract for their entire baseball career, unless traded. The reserve clause put players at an extreme disadvantage when negotiating contracts with teams since they could not test their worth against offers from multiple buyers. Within the field of economic theory, this kind of single-buyer market is called a monopsony, and it had the effect of stifling salaries within professional baseball until the U.S. Supreme Court found that the reserve clause constituted an illegal restraint of trade.[11] Further strengthening the hand of owners, Major League Baseball enjoys a unique exemption from all federal antitrust legislation, something that they have enjoyed since a U.S. Supreme Court ruling granted them this privilege in 1912. As a result, baseball team owners have the ability to block any new league from establishing teams that might compete for player contracts.

From the time that the reserve clause was established, it created friction between owners and players. In 1885, players, led by New York Giants pitcher John Montgomery Ward, created the first baseball union, the Brotherhood of Professional Base Ball Players, in response to the reserve clause and its use by baseball team owners. In 1890, Brotherhood players even attempted to stage a revolt and create their own league. Even though the league collapsed within a year, it illustrates the depth of the conflict between players and owners that was created by the reserve clause and the degree to which it was part of a structural tension within major league labor relations.[12]

In 1969, Curt Flood of the St. Louis Cardinals challenged the legality of the reserve clause when he refused to accept a trade to the Philadelphia Phillies. He lost his case, but with the backing of the newly formed Major League Baseball Players Association, led by lawyer Marvin Miller, the players revived their challenge to the reserve clause. Players first showed their solidarity during a short strike in 1972 over the player benefit plan that delayed the start of the season by ten days. By 1975, they had focused their grievance with owners and once more had taken the case of the reserve clause to the U.S. Supreme Court. This time, the justices came down in favor of the players, and the reserve clause was lifted.

As "free agents," players could now put their skills on the auction block for the highest bidder, and the results were dramatic. At the time of this landmark ruling in 1975, the average player salary was $61,000, $1,539,000 less than the average player salary during the 1994 season. Owners, along with many sportswriters and fans, have tended to blame this rise in salaries upon the lifting of the reserve clause, creating a phenomenon that has pejoratively been called "free agency." It might be more accurate to look at the salary discrepancy as evidence of how much the reserve clause artificially suppressed salaries during the time in which it was a standard part of a player's contract.

However one might think about it, elimination of the reserve clause opened the door for players and owners to more equitably distribute shares of baseball revenues. As Paul Staudohar points out, the size of the baseball pie is actually not very big as compared to revenues for productive industries like automobile manufacturing in the United States. However, between the players and the owners, there are also not very many people seeking a piece of this pie (at the time of the strike, about 750 players and twenty-eight owners). While small when compared to other industries, baseball has gained billions in net income through television revenues, money from tickets and luxury boxes, and various licensing agreements. Thus, a great deal is at stake to each side when baseball owners and players sit down to hammer out an agreement.[13]

The 1994–1995 strike had its most immediate roots in the 1990 "lockout," when owners proposed a severe restructuring of the baseball collective bargaining agreement. The main sticking point to that proposal had been a salary cap that would limit the amount of money each team could pay to all of its players. Fearful that players would strike late in the season, owners chose to preemptively close training camps in the spring for thirty-two days. The tactic failed, and the owners lost this first battle. However, in December 1992, owners decided to reopen negotiations over the issue of free agency. Once again, the talks failed to reach a resolution, and in the midst of the brewing confrontation between owners and players, Commissioner Faye Vincent resigned.[14]

As owners were failing to bring about an agreement that restricted the free agency of players, they were dealt another economic blow. In the early 1990s, it was becoming clear that baseball was losing much of its popularity among fans, especially those who watched the game on television. Low ratings for regular season, playoff, and World Series games led to a loss of over $500 million by CBS and $150 million by ESPN, leading these networks in 1993 to cut back their agreements with Major League Baseball's ownership. Major League Baseball teams now were getting only about half of the money that they used to get from the networks. Network television money is evenly shared among major league teams, so those franchises in the smallest markets, least able to make up the loss of revenue with local television contracts or gate receipts, were the hardest hit by this new situation. What is more, such teams found themselves committed to expensive long-term player contracts that they could no longer afford under the terms of the new television deal.[15]

Fearful that the owners would unilaterally impose a salary cap when the old collective bargaining agreement expired at the end of the season, players elected to strike on August 12, a date that harmed owners as much as possible. In the end, the strike would last 232 days, extending into the start of the 1995 season and commanding the attention of everyone from the House of Representatives to the president of the United States. The final agreement included almost no changes to the basic principle of free agency except for a "luxury tax" imposed upon owners who exceeded a maximum team salary payroll.

The Major League Baseball strike of 1994–1995 is something that many fans continue to remember. In fact, the year 1994 was characterized to a great extent by resentment and anger expressed by what became known as "angry white men" that has had a lasting political impact. Bonding over a perceived decline in moral certainty and "traditional values," many rallied around the conservative political rhetoric of right-wing radio talk show hosts like Rush Limbaugh.

The baseball strike that cut short the 1994 season may not have caused this anger, but it certainly contributed to it. Among such fans, there was little patience for the messy realities of baseball's past labor relations or the intricacies of its present economic battles. Baseball represented yet one more American institution that had become "corrupted." Within such a context, a powerful, successful, wealthy, and cocky African American player like Barry Bonds became a symbol of the game's corruption. It would become an image that Bonds would have trouble shaking throughout his subsequent career.

NOTES

1. Michael Wilbon, "Baseball Gets Charged with a Costly Error," *Washington Post*, August 13, 1994, F1.

2. "Sports News," Associated Press, September 22, 1993.

3. Gene Seymour, "Golden Turkeys XI, for Your Thanksgiving Day Dining Pleasure," *(Springfield, IL) State Journal-Register*, November 24, 1994, 42; Hal Brock, "Sports News," Associated Press, December 24, 1994.

4. Richard Cole, "Sports News," Associated Press, May 16, 1995.

5. "Baseball Notes," *Washington Post*, August 22, 2000; "Sports News," Associated Press, October 9, 2001.

6. Michael Holly, "Strange Days," *Boston Globe*, December 26, 1995, 39.

7. Tim Keown, "It Was All about Money and Violence," *San Francisco Chronicle*, December 25, 1995, B1.

8. "His Agent Part (Bad) Company," *Pittsburgh Post-Gazette*, January 26, 1992, D2; Carol Herwig, "Baseball," *USA Today*, December 29, 1992, 11C; Wendy E. Lane, "Sports News," Associated Press, October 21, 1993.

9. "Bonds Could Lose Plenty," *Montreal Gazette*, March 1, 1995, D1.

10. Bob Levin, "Mean Season," *McLean's*, September 26, 1994.

11. Paul Staudohar, "The Baseball Strike of 1994–95," *Monthly Labor Review* 120, no. 3, March 1997, 21–28.

12. Staudohar, "The Baseball Strike of 1994–95," 21–28; David Q. Voigt, *America through Baseball* (New York: Nelson Hall, 1976), 205–216.

13. Staudohar, "The Baseball Strike of 1994–95," 21–28.

14. Ibid.

15. Ibid.

5

A Target of Resentment, 1995–1999

Talk radio hosts of the mid-1990s, presuming to speak for the "angry white men" of the nation, often directed their rage toward the federal government. Agents from the Federal Bureau of Investigation and the Bureau of Alcohol, Tobacco, and Firearms were labeled "jack-booted thugs" for affronting the rights of nongovernmental militias and fundamentalist Christian or white supremacist organizations like the Michigan Militia, the Branch Dividians, and the Freedmen. Even those who were not on this reactionary fringe talked of "getting the government off our back," paying lower taxes, and unreasonable federal mandates. Ironically, however, it was the federal government that, in the end, forced the end of the baseball strike.

At the end of 1994, with the expiration of the old collective bargaining agreement with players, owners imposed the new rules that they had hoped to convince players to accept, the most important of which was a salary cap, or a limitation on the total amount of money any team could keep on its player payroll. The players' union filed a grievance with the National Labor Relations Board (NLRB), arguing that the owners had imposed unilateral conditions of employment without a good-faith effort to negotiate. The NLRB agreed on March 26, 1995, just days before the official starting date of the baseball season. Five days later, U.S. District Court judge Sonia Sotomayer ruled in favor of the NLRB, and imposed a preliminary injunction against the owners. The old agreement between owners and players was reinstated, the owners decided not to lock out the players, and the players' union agreed to go back to work. By late April, Major League Baseball was back in business, en route to a strike-shortened 144-game season.[1]

Fans, however, did not necessarily return to baseball. Attendance in 1995 dropped by 20 percent from the previous year, and many vowed never to come back to baseball. Teams did work to bring them to the ballpark through a variety of gimmicks and schemes. The San Francisco Giants tried offering free tickets to all children under 14, for example. For the Giants, however, ticket giveaways were not enough. Their season attendance at Candlestick Park dropped from a record 2.6 million in 1993 to 1.24 million in 1995. According to the team ownership, as a result of the strike year and the resulting loss in attendance, the Giants would lose more than $45 million between 1994 and 1998.[2]

Not surprisingly, early in the new season following the end of the strike, Barry Bonds made comments to the local media that incited anger. During a game in early June, Bonds failed to chase after a fly ball that was hit in his direction, thinking that the ball was a sure home run. This came shortly after Bonds failed to run out a fly ball that he had hit. Responding to hostile fans after his two miscues, Bonds snapped at reporters, saying, "I don't care what they [the fans] think. They don't know what's going on. They don't bother me. If they can do better, bring their [butt] out there and do it."[3]

Later, Bonds apologized for his outburst. "I just snapped," he told reporters. "It was wrong on my part. I should have kept myself in control, been a stronger person about it." Bonds noted that the strains of his contentious divorce proceedings may have contributed to his anger. "I'm on deck and somebody is saying something about alimony. How do I explain that to my son? I don't think it was toward the fans. I messed up a play in left field. That's the first time that's ever happened. I was mad at myself at what happened."[4]

Bonds' apology was too little, too late for many, as his comment provoked a flurry of angry mail from local fans in the Bay Area. Explaining why fans were staying away from the ballpark, Ron Horne of Kentfield, California, wrote to the *San Francisco Chronicle*, "Barry Bonds' latest example of fan derision finally did me in. Watching him look blandly away from his fans as he fulfills his daily chore of signing autographs and listening to him justify his lack of hustle as he earns his $48,611 daily salary is just unbearable." Chris Cooney of San Francisco wrote in, "Barry, I might not be a better baseball player than you, but I'm definitely not as lazy and conceited. And if the Giants offered me one one-hundredth of the salary, I'd gladly put on your uniform and show you how to do your job." D. W. Page of Santa Rosa quipped, "[W]hat's the big deal about Barry Bonds not running to catch a fly ball to the outfield? He never runs when he hits a fly ball to the outfield, either."[5] Tim Keown of the *Chronicle* wrote,

> The fallout from the baseball strike continues to land in unlikely places. Experts everywhere attempted to predict the biggest single ef-

fect of the strike, but now it appears everybody was wrong. Some said the pitching would be ahead of the hitting, and some said the opposite. Some said the fan response would be most telling, but even that has been superseded by one remarkable phenomenon: Barry Bonds' depth perception.

Bonds apparently thinks everything's going out, whether he hits it or someone else does. And you've heard it before, but it's worth repeating: If you think you can do better, he'll apologize tomorrow.[6]

Keown goes on to quote Giants broadcaster Mike Krukow, who, after Bonds failed to run out his fly ball, said, "The mustard came off the hot dog once this series, and it did it again. You've got to stop doing that."[7] Two years earlier, Bonds was a league Most Valuable Player, drawing a record number of fans to games and leading his team to 103 wins. In 1995, the Giants finished ten games under the .500 mark, and although Bonds had very good numbers (33 home runs, 104 RBIs, .294 batting average, .577 slugging percentage) and even led the league in on-base percentage, it would be one of only two seasons between 1990 and 2003 that he would not finish in the top ten in Most Valuable Player voting. Letters to editors and the text of sports columns reveal a steady pattern of thought—Barry Bonds was an example of everything wrong with baseball. As baseball fan Mark Hurley of New York put it when he wrote into the *Sporting News* that spring, "I don't care what happens to the ever-moody Barry Bonds. . . . Baseball is dead. And with the bunch that is running and playing the sport, good riddance."[8]

One of the more interesting patterns in fan and media criticism of Bonds is the perception that he is lazy. This perception was largely at the core of fans' anger over Bonds' failure to run out the grounder and chase the fly ball. Those actions certainly cost the team the chance to get a base runner and an opportunity to prevent a run, yet they also reinforced the notion that Bonds did not hustle, that he relied upon his natural abilities and talents, and that other players played harder and worked harder. Most reporters and players who know Bonds well report that this is far from an accurate description of the star.

In fact, for most of his career, Bonds has been known as one of the best-conditioned, best-prepared, and hardest-working players in the game, by both those who like and dislike him. In his interview for this book, *Oakland Tribune* sportswriter Josh Suchon noted that Bonds undergoes a training regimen during the off-season that is so strenuous, other major leaguers who have joined him have had trouble keeping up with his pace.[9] Even early in his career, in the midst of their public conflict during the Pirates spring training camp, Bonds' manager Jim Leyland vigorously defended Bonds' work ethic. Nevertheless, statements about Bonds being a "loafer," and a "hot dog" had been part of his profile since he first came to the major leagues, but they say much more about public perceptions of Bonds than they do about him as a real person. *Chronicle* sports columnist C. W. Nevius articulated this image of Bonds in a column that was printed shortly after the fly-ball episode.

> He is not a leader, on or off the field. He declines to bother with mandatory team stretching before many games, and he has exasperated generations of old-school baseball fans by refusing to run out routine ground balls because he feels the pointless effort takes too much out of him. . . . That's the Barry Bonds that baseball will know. As his skills erode, Bonds says that he will play out his contract, which runs through 2000, and fade away. If so, he will be known as a player who was just a notch below the greats—talented but mercurial, an odd guy who often annoyed his teammates and always mystified them. Nice numbers, though.[10]

When one of the hardest-working players in baseball is repeatedly labeled lazy, it is worth investigating what may be behind such a charge. The character of this resentment is one that is often disproportionately directed toward African American athletes, and it is a frequent criticism of talented African American baseball players. From George Bell to Albert Belle, from Dick Allen to Ricky Henderson, from Curt Flood to Reggie Jackson, from Bobby Bonds to Barry Bonds, and even going as far back as Jackie Robinson and Larry Doby, sportswriters and fans have directed an inordinate amount of scorn upon black baseball players who express too much individual flair, or who simply seem very self-confident and arrogant.

Many of these players certainly have behaved in ways that may have invited scorn, yet so have many white baseball players who do not seem to have been defined by their unseemly actions in quite the same way. The consistent pattern of such criticism, even when it contradicts the facts, suggests that it may say as much about those who level it as it does about those toward whom it is directed. In particular, the characterization of African American athletes as lazy is something that has a long history to it, one that goes well beyond even the existence of professional sports. Such images are part of what cultural studies scholar Stuart Hall calls a "racialized regime of representation."[11]

During the middle of the nineteenth century, when abolitionists first began to seriously challenge the institution of slavery in the United States, defenders of slavery repeatedly supported the institution by evoking images of "inherent" differences between blacks and whites, particularly of white supremacy and black inferiority. Seeking to stir up white fears of intermarriage, inbreeding, and revenge, proslavery propagandists portrayed people of African descent as the embodiment of "savagery" who needed to be controlled by white "civilization." If not under the sternest forms of white control, blacks were said to retreat into unrestrained sexuality, an ethic that highlighted the pursuit of pleasure, and a social organization guided by barbarism and undisciplined anarchy.[12]

Hall notes that one of the major themes to emerge out of the debate over slavery was that of the " 'innate laziness' of blacks—'naturally' born to, and fitted only for, servitude but, at the same time, stubbornly unwilling to labor in ways appropriate to their nature and profitable for their masters."[13] Ultimately, of course, defenders of slavery lost, and the institution was abolished in the United States, yet the images and stereotypes that developed during the era of slavery continued to circulate and get rearticulated in different forms over the course of generations. For example, Hall cites Donald Bogle's work showing how early stereotypes of blacks have lived on in Hollywood films. Among the five main images that Bogle defines is that of the "Bad Buck," "physically big, strong, no-good, violent, renegades, 'on a rampage and full of black rage,' 'over-sexed and savage, violent and frenzied as they lust for white flesh.' "[14]

This last image has resonated powerfully with representations of black athletes, particularly as, over the past fifty years, people of the African Diaspora have gained access to, and come to dominate, many high-profile sports. Hall, for example, notes how it became a conventional part of media stories about Ben Johnson during the 1988 Olympics after Johnson tested positive for having used performance-enhancing drugs to win the 100-meter gold medal race.[15] It is also a stereotype that has resonated with moments of controversy in Bonds' career: his confrontation with Jim Leyland; his divorce from Sue; his battles with teammate Jeff Kent; and his alleged connection with steroids. Whether or not it was actually true, it was an image that had a history that preceded Bonds and that many white fans—seeing with anger over the prolonged baseball strike and emboldened by the era's popular image of "angry white male"—were ready to believe. It is also a stereotype that would follow Bonds during his dramatic renaissance between 2000 and 2003, when the strength of Bonds on-field performance was matched only by the viciousness of his critics.

Ironically, despite the fact that he was portrayed as a selfish baseball player, Bonds became perhaps one of the most powerful franchise players during his tenure with the San Francisco Giants in the 1990s. This can be taken quite literally given the central role that Bonds played in resurrecting the Giants franchise in San Francisco. In December 1995, the team ownership announced its plan to build a new stadium for the Giants to replace Candlestick Park, or as it had become renamed, 3-Com Park. The Giants ownership promised that the proposed new stadium would be everything that Candlestick Park had not been:

cozy and charming, easily accessible (located adjacent to San Francisco's downtown), and protected from wind.

In fact, long before the baseball strike, the Giants had a tremendous problem attracting fans to games largely because of their baseball stadium. Fans, players, and owners could all agree that Candlestick Park was one of the most miserable places to watch a major league contest in the United States. Built in 1960 as a modern home for the newly relocated team from New York, Candlestick stands on a landfill lot near the city's southeastern frontier—a place that happened to be in one of the foggiest, windiest, and coldest microclimates in a city known for its summertime fog, wind, and cold. For years, under three different owners, the Giants public relations management heroically struggled to give their fans the illusion that sitting through nine innings of baseball in freezing cold weather and high winds while cupping one's hands around a Styrofoam cup of coffee could actually be considered entertainment.

Originally built as a partially enclosed, baseball-only ballpark, it was praised during its opening season as the greatest stadium ever built by none other than Richard Nixon. Of course, both the future president and the ballpark would become disgraced in a matter of time, but it took only about a year for Candlestick's deficiencies to become exposed when, during the 1961 All Star Game, in front of a national television audience, the wind would blow pitcher Stu Miller off the mound in the top of the ninth inning. The umpire called him for a balk, and the American League scored the go-ahead run.[16]

When the San Francisco 49ers National Football League team moved into Candlestick, the city of San Francisco decided to enclose the stadium to make it better suited for football. Many hoped that the enclosure would cut down on the winds. After the construction was completed in 1972, everybody discovered that the new architectural appendage actually only made the gusts swirl around more in the fashion of a tornado. Usually during the sixth or seventh innings of a typical day game, play would have to be momentarily suspended as a dust devil kicked up from the sliding pads located between the Astroturf base paths, blowing grit into the eyes of batters and shortstops, and hot dog wrappers into the masks of the catcher and umpire. In the ten seasons between 1968 and 1977, the team managed to draw over 1 million fans only once. During the 1974 and 1975 seasons, the Giants barely managed to draw *one-half* a million fans, leading team owner Horace Stoneham to attempt to sell the team to an ownership that would move the franchise to the comparatively warmer climate of Toronto. The stands at Candlestick were so sparsely populated during the 1970s that a shout from adolescent fans could be heard clearly behind Lon Simmons' sleepy play-by-play, so much so that parents of these youngsters could recognize their children's voices and rest assured that their kids had arrived at the game safely. Between 1974 and 1977, the team averaged 7,314 fans per game.

Not surprisingly, the Giants ownership had lobbied for years to get a new stadium built for their team. Doing so, however, would require public money, and San Francisco voters were not inclined to spend their tax dollars to build a stadium for their baseball team. In a city like San Francisco that was thriving economically and attracting tourists even without a successful baseball team, it was hard to argue that a publicly financed stadium was truly necessary. Voters rejected bids to publicly finance new ballparks in the city of San Francisco in 1987 and 1989, despite the fact that the team went to the postseason in each of those years. Voters in Santa Clara County and San Jose, both south of San Francisco, also rejected stadium propositions in the early 1990s. Before Peter Magowan purchased the Giants in 1993, low attendance and a future at Candlestick once more made it look as if the team might leave the West Coast, this time for either New Orleans or St. Petersburg, Florida.[17]

When Peter Magowan announced his plans to build a new stadium for the team in 1995, it was not a proposal that seemed to require a great deal of public investment. In fact, out of the $357 million required to build the venue in the China Basin area just south of Market Street in San Francisco, Magowan pledged to pay $170 million directly from the Giants, a debt that the team would repay in annual $20 million payments over the course of twenty years. In addition, the team would raise money from a variety of other sources including naming rights; "pouring rights" to the drink concessions; other sponsorships; and "seat licenses"—or a special fee that fans would have to pay for the "right" to buy the best 15,000 seats in the ballpark. These other sources of revenue would amount to roughly another $172 million.[18]

Despite the fact that much of the money to build the new ballpark would come from private sources, voters needed to approve the plan since it involved a zoning exemption. In addition, led by Mayor Willie Brown, the city offered to provide "increment financing" to the Giants to the tune of $10 million, using a portion of the increased property taxes that the stadium would purportedly generate to finance its construction.[19] On March 26, 1996, by a margin of 66 to 34 percent, San Francisco voters approved the Giants plans to build a new home for the team. Team president and managing general partner Magowan told a crowd during a victory rally, "Tonight, I feel a little bit like a mommy elephant. . . . This has been a long time in coming."[20]

Designed by HOK Sports, the company that drew up the plans for Oriole Park at Camden Yards, the new stadium would hold 42,000 fans, considerably smaller than Candlestick's 60,000 seating capacity. Almost custom-built for left-handed power hitters like Bonds, the outfield wall would be placed only 307 feet down the right-field line. A 335-foot home run over the brick edifice would land in a small pocket of San Francisco Bay that the Giants would name Mc-Covey Cove (after Willie McCovey, who starred at first base for the Giants in the 1960s and 1970s). To display the drama of this feature, the team had pitcher Shawn Estes throw to Bonds at the groundbreaking for the new stadium on December 11, 1997. Hitting from the approximate spot where home plate would be, Bonds sent the first of many long fly balls into the chilly water.[21]

However charming it might have been and however much it improved the quality of watching a baseball game for fans, it is less clear how important baseball stadiums and professional sports franchises are to a city and its economy. Shortly before winning the voters over in 1995, Peter Magowan uttered the familiar mantra repeated among sports team owners and downtown boosters in a variety of U.S. cities—that sports franchises and public funds that support them are good for the local economy. Magowan said, "Nothing comes easily in San Francisco. It's a skeptical, fragmented city. It took 20 years to decide to build the Golden Gate Bridge. But after the fabulous success of ballparks in Baltimore, Cleveland, and Denver, people can see that something can be good for the economy, which appeals to nonsports fans, and still be nice for fans."[22]

As sports sociologist D. Stanley Eitzen points out, most economic studies of "the economic impact of a stadium and a professional team show consistently that sport has a negligible impact on metropolitan economies."[23] In fact, Eitzen, George Lipsitz, and many others have argued that state subsidies for sports stadium construction amount to a massive redistribution of wealth from the poorest sectors of society to the most affluent. In cities such as Pittsburgh and St. Louis, teams have asked for and received tens of millions of dollars in taxpayer funds and municipal bonds at the very moment when their school budgets have faced severe shortfalls. The same year that the citizens of San Francisco approved their stadium deal (which did contain hidden costs to taxpayers), the federal government cut $55 billion in aid to the poor.[24]

Even though Pac Bell Park was built drawing a large portion of its financing from the Giants ownership, it is not necessarily an exception to the rule that sports stadiums transfer wealth upward. When Peter Magowan and the Giants finish paying off the mortgage on their stadium (a mortgage that will actually account for less than half the amount of money it cost to build the structure), they will own it. This means that the team will have an extremely valuable piece of commercial real estate in a city where the financial worth of such properties is at a premium. Given the fact that the stadium will be an extremely valuable property asset, the public of San Francisco assumed a remarkable degree of the risk required to construct it—the special "increment financing" that the city gave the team, the municipal bonds that San Francisco floated (providing tax-free interest to its creditors), and the zoning exemptions that the stadium required. Policies like those promoting public aid to baseball team owners/supermarket executives seeking help in the financing of privately owned baseball stadiums have led to perhaps the largest gap in wealth distribution in the United States since the Gilded Age of the late nineteenth and early twentieth centuries.

Here we can see the importance of Bonds to the team's long-term strategic vision. The vast majority of voters do not have the time or patience to investigate the complex economic costs and benefits of sports stadiums, particularly ones with intricate financing schemes like Pac Bell Park. Considering that the voters in the Bay Area had rejected four previous bids by the Giants to build a new ballpark, the value of a marquee player like Barry Bonds is extremely important. He lends a winning image to a team that for years had lacked it. Conversely, Bonds also benefited by supporting and helping to promote the new stadium. In the shell game that transfers wealth from ordinary citizens of a city like San Francisco to wealthy individuals and corporations, high-profile athletes like Bonds are winners. Increased wealth for the Giants has meant that the team can continue to pay his high salary (even though the front office continually complains about having to keep a low payroll so it can afford its mortgage payments).

Thus, it was no coincidence that the groundbreaking for Pac Bell Park would focus upon Bonds. He was a critical reason that the Giants could even think of winning a referendum to build a new stadium in San Francisco. The team front office even postponed negotiations with Bonds over a restructuring of this contract until after the vote had taken place. It was as if to tell the voters that if they wanted to keep Barry, they had better build him a house. As much as he drew the ire of angry fans, he attracted people to the ballpark to see him play, and he made it possible for fans to think of the team as a potential contender. Even during the 1996 season, when the team lost ninety-four games and finished twenty-three games out of first place, Bonds and the Giants managed to attract more than 1.4 million fans through the turnstiles of 3-Com (formerly Candlestick) Park.

For Giants management to break even while paying for their new stadium, they estimated that they would need to attract an average of 3 million fans a season. This was a tall order for a team that, exactly twenty years earlier, had an average attendance of almost 6,500 per game. With Bonds as the star attraction, however, this was not out of the realm of possibility. *San Francisco Chronicle* sports columnist David Steele notes that Bonds' presence was integral to a revival of the franchise that included the new ownership, the hiring of Dusty Baker, and the building of the new ballpark. Steele remembers, "The Giants were pretty much dead before they all came. What's all happened now with these guys is a phenomenon of the last ten years. You know, they were on their way out of town. They basically had flopped. The franchise was dead in San Francisco. The fact that it has turned out the way it has is a miracle almost."[25]

One other player on the Giants was considered important to the team's future, third baseman Matt Williams. In 1994, Williams was on pace to break the single-season home-run record, at that time still held by Roger Maris, when the strike ended baseball for the year. Many fans thought that Williams was an essential complement to Bonds in the Giants line-up.

Nevertheless, at the end of the 1996 season, Giants first-year general manager Brian Sabean engineered a trade that sent Williams to the Cleveland Indians for a relatively unknown infielder named Jeff Kent. Fans were incredulous. Williams seemed like an essential component of the team. For those with memories long enough, the move must have brought back memories of some of the other Giants superstars who went on to fabulous careers on other teams: Orlando Cepeda, George Foster, Gary Mathews, Gary Maddox, Gaylord Perry, and, of course, Bobby Bonds, just to name a few. Angry callers who phoned a local sports talk show with Sabean as a guest prompted the new team executive to tell listeners, "I'm not an idiot. I know what I'm doing."[26]

Kent would not only show that Sabean was not an idiot but make him look like a genius. In fact, the trade for Kent, who ended up winning the National League Most Valuable Player award in 2000 and who helped lead the team to three playoff appearances and a National League pennant, was a perfect one for the team's on-field performance. With Bonds batting third and Kent batting cleanup, the two players complemented each other perfectly. Unfortunately, Kent and Bonds did not mix as well when it came to their relationship off the field.

The son of a police officer and native of a conservative Orange County, California, suburb, Kent, like Bonds, had a reputation for being a difficult personality. He starred in high school and at the University of California, Berkeley, helping the team to a regional title and a spot in the College World Series in 1988. His early years in the major leagues were relatively unimpressive. He had a reputation for making errors and for not having enough speed to play effectively at his preferred position of second base. Yet with the Giants, he blossomed. During his first season with the team, he hit a modest .250, but his 29 home runs and 121 RBIs were crucial to the team down the stretch. That year, they would go from having the worst record in the National League in 1996 to the division title and a playoff spot against the Florida Marlins, who would eventually win the World Series.[27]

In their years together as teammates, Bonds and Kent would have their share of flare-ups, but for the most part, their animosity was reflected in a generally cold indifference toward one another. As Suchon puts it,

From day one, Kent and Bonds were never friends. That isn't exactly shocking. They both keep to themselves. Neither is considered "one of the boys." If they disliked each other, it never came out publicly, unless you happened to ask Kent if he saw better pitches hitting behind Bonds. The most telling sign, if any, was Kent's often indifference or token handshakes after Bonds hit a homer.[28]

In 1997, however, whatever personality differences existed between Kent and Bonds were of secondary importance. By August, it was apparent that the Giants were, in fact, a contender to make the postseason for the first time since 1989. Leading the team were a staff of capable young starting pitchers Shawn Estes and Kirk Rueter, complemented by veteran Mark Gardner. The Giants bullpen was also strong, anchored by Julian Tavarez (picked up from Cleveland in the Matt Williams trade) and closer Rod Beck. Throughout much of the season, Bonds did not perform at the plate as well as he had in the past. However, Jeff Kent ended up doing far better than expected, hitting 29 home runs, and batting in 121 runs. At first base, J. T. Snow also drove in over 100 runs after being acquired by the Giants in a trade with Anaheim during the preseason. With Bonds' 101 runs batted in, Snow, Kent, and Bonds became the first Giants to drive in 100 runs each in a season since Johnny Mize, Walker Cooper, and Willard Marshall in 1947. Fans began to consider that perhaps Brian Sabean was not an idiot after all.[29]

In August, Bonds had trouble getting hits when runners were on base. By September, however, fans and sportswriters noticed a change in his energy level, which was also revealed in his performance. Getting clutch hits during a torrid playoff stretch in September, he ended up hitting .291 with 40 home runs. Tim Keown, writing for the *San Francisco Chronicle*, noted at the end of the season, "His resurgence occurred just as he was beginning to hear boos, and just as the team wondered if he would ever come around." Demonstrating the patience at the plate that would become his trademark during the remainder of his career, he also drew 145 walks. During a key stretch of 9 games at the end of the season, Bonds hit 7 home runs, hit 3 doubles, scored 12 times, and drove in 13 runs. The Giants ended up coming from 2 games behind the Dodgers at the end of the season to take the National League Western Division pennant. Even Jeff Kent praised Bonds' performance. "Barry's been a big part of this all year," he said. "You don't hit 40 homers and drive in 100 runs without being a big part of it. It just can't happen." Keown wrote, "The last month of the season, Bonds was emotional, exuberant, alive. Nobody knows what took so long, and the Giants are simply glad it happened. The distance from the field to the top of the dugout isn't much, but when Bonds made the trip, he traveled a long way. Suddenly, he was not aloof. Suddenly, he was giving the people what they've been waiting for—emotion, excitement, a sense that he is one of them."[30]

Bonds was finally going to the postseason with the Giants. As much as winning the division title, he also had the opportunity to shed his reputation as a player who could not deliver when it counted in the playoffs. Bonds had developed that reputation as an outfielder with the Pirates. In the Florida Marlins, the Giants playoff opponents, Bonds was facing the two people with whom he played in Pittsburgh whom he most respected: his former manager and mentor, Jim Leyland, and slugger Bobby Bonilla. Bonilla also had not been spectacular in the playoffs as a Pirate, and after going 4 for 35 with the Baltimore Orioles in the 1996 playoffs, he entered the series with the Giants sporting a .190 lifetime postseason batting average, yet in this best-of-five series, the pressure seemed to be on Bonds. Paul Meyer, writing for the *Pittsburgh Post-Gazette*, noted that the 1997 playoffs seemed to be haunted by the ghosts of Pittsburgh's past disappointments. "If Bonds produces as he did in the final three games of the '92 series, the Marlins could be toast. But if Bonds produces as he did in his other 17 postseason games, he'll be roasted. Again. 'I don't really care what anyone thinks about it,' Bonds said of his putrid postseason numbers. 'I go out there and try, that's all. Whatever people want to write, they'll write.' Here's what a lot of people will write today. That in 20 postseason games with the Pirates, Bonds was 13 for 68 (.191) with one home run and three RBIs. With runners in scoring position, he was 1 for 19. With runners on base, he was 2 for 33."[31]

Unfortunately for Bonds, it would be yet another October of frustration. In the opening game, the Giants lost 2–1. Bonds had one hit in four at-bats, and his frustration could be sensed in his quip to reporters, "I finally got a hit." After losing again in the second game, the Giants returned to San Francisco to lose the third game 6–2 on a sixth-inning grand slam by Devon White. In the bottom of the sixth, Bonds had a chance to help his team come back after Bill Mueller opened with a single. Bonds, however, struck out on a 3–2 pitch. Mueller, running on the pitch, was tagged out at second on a throw from Marlins catcher Charles Johnson. The Giants were swept in their best-of-five game series against Florida, and in their three games played, Bonds managed only three hits in twelve at-bats.[32]

Nevertheless, Bonds was more optimistic than ever about the Giants prospects in the future. In a quote that would have made Yogi Berra proud, he told reporters, "If we stay the same, it's going to get better."[33] The Giants would once again be in contention for a playoff spot the following year, one in which excitement for baseball was ignited when Mark McGwire of the St. Louis Cardinals and Sammy Sosa of the Chicago Cubs raced each other past the single-season home-run mark, a race that McGwire won by hitting number 70 during his team's last game. The Cubs, however, would go to the postseason, edging the Giants in a single-game playoff for the final wild card spot. Despite losing to the Cubs, San Francisco had finally put together back-to-back winning seasons, and they looked as if they might be a contending team for years to come.

Off the field, Bonds also generated fewer negative headlines as the decade came to a close. On January 10, 1998, he married a longtime friend, Liz Watson. Together, they had a daughter, Aisha Lynn, Bonds' third child after his son Nikolai and daughter Shikari from his previous marriage to Sun. Those close to Bonds said that he had never seemed more relaxed and stable in his personal life. "Ever since I got married [to Liz]," Bonds later recalled, "I've had the best years of my career. That's my soul mate."[34]

To the press, Bonds became more open and engaging, and he worked hard to improve his image among fans, yet his troubles were not through. In 1999, Bonds for the first time suffered an injury that kept him out of the line-up for an extended period of time. He hit only .262 in 102 games that year, and the Giants ended the season 13½ games out of first place. When the Giants opened their season in 2000 in brand-new Pac Bell Park, many openly wondered if, at 35, Bonds' best days were behind him.

NOTES

1. Staudohar, "The Baseball Strike of 1994–95," 21–28.

2. Suchon, *This Gracious Season*, 70–71.

3. Mark Camps, "Barry Says 'I'm Sorry' to Fans," *San Francisco Chronicle*, June 7, 1995, D3.

4. Ibid.

5. D. W. Page, "Letters to the Green," *San Francisco Chronicle*, June 10, 1995, B2.

6. T. M. Keown, "Barry Bonds Is Deep in Thought," *San Francisco Chronicle*, June 10, 1995, B3.

7. Ibid.

8. Mark Hurley, "Voice of the Fan," *Sporting News*, May 1, 1995.

9. Josh Suchon, interview with author, May 15, 2003.

10. Suchon, *This Gracious Season*, 206–207.

11. Stuart Hall, ed., *Representation: Cultural Representations and Signifying Practices* (Thousand Oaks, CA: Sage, 1997), 232.

12. G. Frederickson, *The Black Image in the White Mind* (Hanover, NH: Wesleyan University Press, 1987), 49; Stuart Hall, ed., *Representation: Cultural Representations and Signifying Practices* (Thousand Oaks, CA: Sage, 1997), 244.

13. Hall, *Representation*, 244.

14. Donald Bogle, *Toms, Coons, Mulattos, Mammies and Bucks: An Interpretive History of Blacks in American Films* (New York: Viking Press, 1973), 6–12.

15. Hall, *Representation*, 226.

16. Suchon, *This Gracious Season*, 69–71.

17. Ibid., 71.

18. Ibid.

19. "Giants Ballpark: Home Run," *San Francisco Examiner*, March 27, 1996, A–1.

20. Ibid.

21. Suchon, *This Gracious Season*, 71.

22. Robert Lipsyte, "Looking to San Francisco Voters to Send Message to Steinbrenner," *New York Times*, March 24, 1996, 8:8.

23. D. Stanley Eitzen, *Fair and Foul: Beyond the Myths and Paradoxes of Sport* (Lanham, MD: Rowman and Littlefield, 2003), 159.

24. Eitzen, *Fair and Foul*, 159; George Lipsitz, "Silence of the Rams: How St. Louis School Children Subsidize the Super Bowl Champs," in *Sports Matters: Race, Recreation, and Leisure*, eds. John Bloom and Michael Nevin Willard (New York: New York University Press, 2002), 225–245.

25. David Steele, interview with author, February 27, 2003.

26. Suchon, *This Gracious Season*, 243.

27. Ibid., 241–242.

28. Ibid., 244.

29. Dennis Georgatos, "Sports News: Giants Hoping to Build on Turnaround Season," Associated Press, October 4, 1997.

30. Time Keown, "How Two Stars Mended Their Ways," *San Francisco Chronicle*, September 30, 1997, E1.

31. Paul Meyer, "Five Years Later," *Pittsburgh Post-Gazette*, September 30, 1997, E1.

32. Ed Price, " 'Football Stadium' Rankles Bonds," *Palm Beach Post*, October 1, 1997, 2C.

33. Dennis Georgatos, "Sports News: Giants Hoping to Build on Turnaround Season."

34. Chuck Johnson, "Bonds-Mays Ties Go Deep," *USA Today*, September 2, 2003, 1C.

CHASING THE BABE IN THE HOUSE THAT BONDS BUILT, 2000–2001

In June 2000, *Sports Illustrated* published its first feature article on Barry Bonds in seven years. It marked the end of Bonds' boycott of the magazine that began after the infamous "I'm Barry Bonds and You're Not" piece in 1993. Although much more sympathetically written, the profile by Jeff Pearlman might have been even more insulting. Pearlman acknowledged in the article that Bonds had an accomplished baseball career and even suggested that Bonds had mellowed into a wiser, more relaxed, and likable person, yet the profile had the tone of an obituary. "Bonds will be 36 in July," Pearlman reminds readers. "When he wakes up the morning after a night game, Bonds's body doesn't scream, Go get 'em! As it once did, but, Go get Advil!" After noting that Bonds had become slower, had gained weight, and had, according to teammate Shawn Estes, lost some of the quickness in his swing, Pearlman opines that, "nothing in sports is sadder to see than the crumbling superstar who, decimated by a couple of incisions and a few misplaced fat cells, has gone from Norm Cash to Casey Candaele, from Tom Seaver to Craig Swan." Pearlman concludes that Bonds is still a great player, even though "in the eyes of many he was displaced as the best player in baseball by Ken Griffey Jr."[1]

No doubt, after the next three seasons, Pearlman would have to profoundly revise his assessment of Bonds' talents, yet he can be forgiven for his premature report of Bonds' demise as a baseball player. The previous season, for the first time in his career, Bonds spent a significant amount of time on the disabled list, losing seven weeks to elbow surgery. The *Sporting News*, in its article and interview with Bonds proclaiming the left fielder the "Baseball Player of the Decade,"

Barry Bonds watches his 73rd home run of the 2001 season leave the park during the first inning of a game against the Los Angeles Dodgers at San Francisco on October 7, 2001. Bonds had broken Mark McGwire's three-year-old single-season home-run mark two days earlier with his 71st home run of the year. © *Reuters/CORBIS.*

noted that Bonds himself was surprised in 1999 to have received the award. "For a brief moment, Bonds, 34, must have forgotten what he has accomplished in the 1990s. He has won three MVP's and eight Gold Gloves and ranks in the top three in home runs, RBI's, slugging percentage and walks." Bonds told the *Sporting News*, "I've never (really analyzed what I have done) because every year is a new challenge. I've never really had time to say, 'My stats for the '90's are better than anybody else's.' I've seen what Ken Griffey Jr. has done throughout the 1990s. Unfortunately, Mark McGwire has been hurt most of the time. If he was healthy, there's no telling what he could have accomplished. . . . One of my favorite players is Mark Grace, and he puts up big numbers every year. My thing has always been a year-to-year basis. Once the year is over, I have moved on to the next year and challenge."[2]

When he arrived at spring training in Arizona in February 2000, Bonds was in a mood to challenge himself. When he sat down with reporters for his first press conference that year, Bonds set what seemed to many to be a ridiculously unrealistic goal. For Josh Suchon, this was his first meeting with Bonds, and it was one that he remembers well.

> Whenever Barry arrives, it's always kind of like, what we call "The State of the Barry," where he talks to the media, basically about every-thing that's going on in his life, or anything that the press can come up with to ask him about what's going on with his life. . . . In the year of 2000, it was a fairly non-eventful year. If I remember cor-rectly, the one thing that he'd said before that year was that he'd been playing around with some numbers in the off-season, and he thought that if he'd had six more good years that he could catch his godfa-ther, Willie Mays, in home runs. That was big news at the time, be-cause that was long before he had hit 73 home runs. At the time, I think he needed to average, I think it was 38 or 39 the next six years, and he was coming off an injury-plagued '99 year, and a lot of people were starting to write Barry off. So I remember there was a lot of de-bate on whether or not he could do it, and the general consensus was there was no way he could do it.[3]

Those reporters might look foolish for discounting such a prediction today, yet nobody could have forecast the most remarkable comeback by a player in major league history. In the four seasons between 2000 and 2003, four seasons that came at what many thought would be the twilight of his career, Barry Bonds became more dominant as a hitter than he had ever been in his life. His cu-mulative batting average over those four seasons is over .334 and his home-run total is 213 (an average of over 50 per season). Bonds' slugging percentage was a career high of .688 in 2000, then soared to a major league record of .863 in 2001. In fact, in 2001, Bonds broke two records held by Babe Ruth—single-season slugging percentage and walks. In 2002 and 2003, Bonds' slugging numbers "dropped off" to .799 and .749, statistics any other player might only dream about as career highs. Having found new patience at the plate, Bonds no longer swung at many pitches that were not in the strike zone, and as a result, he achieved record on-base percentages. Between 2000 and 2003, Bonds was walked, on average, 168 times. When combined with his batting, Bonds had a staggering on-base percentage during these seasons that made him a factor in every game he played, peaking with a .582 average in 2002. In 2001, Bonds shocked the baseball world by hitting a major league record 73 home runs, one set only three seasons earlier by Mark McGwire; and he followed this with his first National League batting title the next season when he hit .370.

As a result of this new prowess, the Giants were once again revived as a baseball team. After a sluggish 1999 season, San Francisco began a revival that would bring the team's performance into that of the major league elite. Yet Bonds also continued to draw as much controversy as praise. He continued to struggle in the playoffs, and despite attempts to rehabilitate his image, he still had a rocky relationship with the press. Sportswriters criticized his personality and speculated about Bonds using performance enhancing drugs.

The Giants began the 2000 season with high hopes. Their brand-new stadium was already a hit with fans and critics, and many hoped that its short right field line would be a hit with Bonds as well. Responding to this enthusiasm, San Francisco left the starting gates in 2000 by losing its first six home games, getting swept in the process by their archrivals, the Los Angeles Dodgers. Ultimately, however the team would redeem itself, winning the Western Division, going to the playoffs, and, along the way, attracting over 3,300,000 fans.

Bonds adjusted well to his new place of work. His 49 home runs that season were a career high. Despite the fact that nearly half of them were hit on the road, Bonds was the only Giant to hit a home run into "McCovey Cove," the small portion of San Francisco Bay beyond the right field wall named after the second greatest left-handed slugger in Giants history, Willie McCovey. Bonds actually hit six home runs into the water. Luis Gonzalez of the Arizona Diamondbacks and Todd Hundley of the Dodgers were the only other players on any opposing team to do so. By October, hopes were high that Pac Bell Park might host a World Series in its first year of operation.[5]

After winning the first game against the Mets, in the first round of post season play the Giants lost three straight, and as in 1997, they got no further than the first round. Bonds managed to get only three hits. With his contract due to expire the following season, rumors began to swirl that the team would do the unthinkable—let Barry go. Many fans reasoned that this was the smartest thing to do. Almost as a foreshadowing of things to come, Bonds came in second in the race for Most Valuable Player in 2000 to Kent. It was a tough decision for sportswriters, and good arguments could be made that either Kent or Bonds deserved the award. However, Bonds felt particularly betrayed because manager Dusty Baker and several Giants teammates publicly supported the decision to give the honor to Kent. Given his age and the amount of money that the team would be free to spend without having to pay off his contract, it looked almost inevitable that Bonds and the Giants would part at the end of 2001.

When Bonds first signed with the Giants in 1992, his contract ran for six seasons. He signed a two-year contract extension in 1999 with an option for 2001, which the Giants exercised, yet as San Francisco opened the year in 2001, they had not signed their superstar left fielder, and general manager Brian Sabean expressed no sense of impatience toward doing so. The team's inaction led many to believe that they would seek a trade for Bonds during the middle of the season. In one of his first moves with San Francisco, Sabean had shocked the baseball world by trading Matt Williams, an exchange in which the Giants obtained then-unheralded second baseman Jeff Kent. It was not beyond the realm of possibility that he would pull off a similar move with Bonds. Superstars Alex Rodriguez and Manny Ramirez had each signed contracts worth $25 million and $20 million, respectively, and if Bonds were to demand that kind of salary, it was clear that the Giants were not willing to pay it. Sabean did not see Bonds as worth an inordinate proportion of the team's payroll. As he told sports reporters after the playoffs in 2000, "If Barry is a free agent at the end of next season, we don't resign him, and we don't get anything in return, that's not going to concern me."[6]

During spring training of 2001, Bonds' agent, Scott Boras, known as one of the most successful and aggressive agents in sports, flew to Arizona to meet with Giants executives. He expressed that Bonds wanted to stay with the Giants and in San Francisco, and Sabean relayed his appreciation for what Bonds had done for the franchise. According to Sabean, the meeting "had an air of diplomacy to it."[7] To reporters, Bonds did seem to be upset that his contract had not been resolved during the off-season, evidenced by the fact that he refused to speak to them during spring training. Other than his silence, however, he showed no other signs that he was having a conflict with the front office. He showed up for camp on time and did not hold out, and he made no public demands that the Giants offer him a salary on the scale of Alex Rodriguez or Manny Ramirez.[8] Perhaps in his silence, Bonds was following the advice of his mentor in Pittsburgh, Jim Leyland, who, years earlier, had advised his young prospect not to become distracted by reporters asking questions about contracts.

This may have been a good strategy, because if one thing was clear in the spring of 2001, it was that the contract issue was not going to be an easy one to resolve. From the perspective of the Giants front office, Bonds, who was earning $10.3 million a year, represented a huge proportion of the team's overall payroll. Just the salaries for Bonds and for closer Rob Nen, another Scott Boras client, took up over a quarter of the team's payroll. Team president Peter Magowan publicly expressed his concern that the team was losing too much money, particularly in light of the $170 million mortgage that they needed to pay for their stadium. Although he wanted to keep the team competitive, he was concerned about maintaining the salaries for players like Bonds, Nen, Kent, first baseman J. T. Snow, and pitcher Shawn Estes. On opening day of 2001, it very much looked as if Bonds, as opposed to all of the other, younger players, would be the one who would have to go.

On opening day of the 2001 season, Bonds had 494 career home runs. Most people who follow baseball consider 500 career home runs a major accomplishment that guarantees one's place in the Hall of Fame. Bonds did not wait long to get started on his chase toward that milepost, hitting number 495 on opening day. In his next 21 at-bats, however, he went hitless, and Bonds was looking less and less relevant to the Giants future. By mid-April, however, Bonds was back on track, and on April 18, against the Dodgers at home, he stood at 499. In the bottom of the eighth, Bonds swung at a 2–0 pitch from Terry Adams and sent it into McCovey Cove. With Giants legends Willie Mays and Willie McCovey on hand to witness the occasion, Bonds circled the bases in triumph, yet what many in the national media focused on later was the lack of celebration by the Giants themselves, most of whom stayed in the dugout.

Those who observed the inaction of his teammates later suggested that it was an illustration of how alienated Bonds had become from his teammates. Suchon, who was covering the game for the *Oakland Tribune*, sees this as an overstatement.

> The truth, as it always is with Barry, isn't black or white. It's gray and imprecise. Many players honestly didn't know whether they were allowed or supposed to come to home plate—or whether they should stay in the dugout. They knew that a brief ceremony was planned for behind home plate and it would involve both Willie's and the Bonds family.[9]

Whatever his fellow players felt about congratulating Bonds, they were certainly happy that the home run won the game, and they must have been happy about how the rest of the season unfolded for their left fielder. By the middle of July, Bonds had hit 40 home runs, and it looked as if he had a realistic chance to break the single-season home-run record of 70 set only three years earlier by Mark McGwire of the St. Louis Cardinals. In fact, in 1998, when McGwire, along with Sammy Sosa of the Chicago Cubs, broke Roger Maris' single-season home-run record of 61, it was an achievement that had stood unchallenged for thirty-seven years. It was almost unthinkable that a record that had taken so long to break could be broken again in such a short period of time. However, as Bonds reached home-run number 51 on August 14, even his greatest critics realized that the goal was within reach. By August 29, Bonds had 56 home runs, and he was at the center of discussion for most of the world that cared about Major League Baseball.

Just as most of the national media focused upon the seemingly apathetic response of his teammates to his 500th career home run, however, much of the coverage of Bonds' single-season home-run chase focused upon his personality. At the All Star Break, when discussion of Bonds' home-run chase was beginning to heat up, Hal Bodley of *USA Today* weighed in on the issue in an article headlined, "Charming Superstar or Selfish Malcontent? It's Up to Bonds." Bodley wrote, "I've felt for years Barry Bonds has trouble figuring out who Barry Bonds is supposed to be. Is he the best player in baseball, whose talents, charisma and charm can overwhelm everyone in his company? Or is he the moody, sometimes bitter young man who detests talking with the media and who'd rather just play his game and to hell with the world?"[10] In late August, Robert Siegel of National Public Radio reported, "Barry Bonds' pursuit of the record is a strange one. The star left-fielder, three-time former National League most valuable player, godson of the sainted Willie Mays and like Mays and his father, Bobby Bonds, one of the rare major-league players who both hits home runs and steals bases with tremendous success. Barry Bonds, despite all this, is just not a very popular hero to the fans." Interviewing *San Francisco Chronicle* reporter Ray Ratto on the air, Siegel noted, "He's certainly a world of difference from, say, McGwire and Sosa or Michael Jordan—or Tiger Woods, for that matter—people who seemed to have just handled stardom a lot more graciously than he has."[11]

In other sports columns that summer, however, Bonds became the target of much more strident criticism, most notably by *Sports Illustrated* columnist Rick Reilly and by esteemed journalist and ESPN.com guest writer David Halberstam. In Halberstam's piece, the writer known for his probing profile into the Kennedy and Johnson administration's growing involvement in the Vietnam War deliberated upon "Why America Will Never Love Barry Bonds." Halberstam concludes that Bonds was the beneficiary of a media makeover that concealed what a truly mean-spirited person he really was. He accuses Bonds not only of "unprovoked, deliberate, gratuitous acts of rudeness towards all kinds of people, other players, [and] distinguished sportswriters," but goes further to place Bonds in a category that might have previously been reserved for the likes of Richard Nixon and J. Edgar Hoover. "This is about nothing less than the abuse of power—he has it by dint of his abilities, and he uses his power to make others' lives more difficult and less pleasant."[12]

Reilly's column painted a familiar portrait of Bonds as a selfish egomaniac, but he did so with added sting by drawing primarily from an interview with Jeff Kent, someone whom most fans interpreted to be Bonds' greatest rival as well as his most important teammate. In an opening line that has become infamous among Barry Bonds fans, Reilly wrote, "In the San Francisco Giants clubhouse, everybody knows the score: 24–1. There are 24 teammates, and there's Barry Bonds." Reilly goes on to note that Bonds failed to show up for the team picture two years in a row; that Bonds refuses to stretch with his teammates before games; that Bonds refuses to take the bus to the ballpark with his teammates; that Bonds has special meals made for him; that Bonds has his own public relations handler; that Bonds has three lockers and a special recliner; and that Bonds does not play cards with his teammates. "Bonds isn't beloved by his teammates," wrote Reilly, "He's not even beliked." Reviving images of Bonds that had driven earlier sportswriters to label Bonds as lazy, Reilly writes, "He often doesn't run out grounders, doesn't run out flies. If a Giants pitcher gives up a monster home run over Bonds in left field, Bonds keeps his hands on his knees and merely swivels his head to watch the ball sail over the fence." Reilly ends by quoting Kent, " 'On the field, we're fine . . . but off the field, I don't care about Barry and Barry doesn't care about me. [Pause.] Or anybody else.' "[13]

As Suchon writes, Bonds chose not to escalate the feud by countering with an attack on Kent. Instead, he suggested that comments can be easily taken out of context and told reporters to consult with Kent if they wanted to know what he meant by his statements to Reilly. Suchon notes, however, that the items Reilly used to criticize Bonds were particularly strange. For example, with regard to Bonds' refusal to ride the bus with teammates, Suchon notes that "most players take a taxi to the park."[14]

Three years earlier, the story in baseball had been the friendly, fun-loving rivalry between Mark McGwire and Sammy Sosa for the home-run record and title. In 2001, the national story seemed to be much more like the one Roger Maris faced in 1961—that the media and many fans had grown to dislike the person about to break the record. In fact, Halberstam's piece echoes the coverage of that home-run chase. In 1961, reporters from around the country were enamored with Maris' teammate Mickey Mantle, a charismatic, fun-loving player who was cast as the rightful heir to Babe Ruth's legacy. Similarly, Halberstam compares Bonds to McGwire and Sosa.

> Three years ago, when Sammy Sosa and McGwire put on their Maris chase, it was great fun. They were perfectly cast, McGwire representing the older, white America, the old-fashioned power hitter as bruiser . . . , Sosa the champion of non-white America, like so many of today's great players, a child of Latin America. . . . They both played it out not merely with considerable grace but with a certain elemental joy; they handled the appalling media demands exceptionally well, as if it were not some terrible unwanted intrusion on their otherwise busy schedules inflicted by a a hostile federal judge, behaving instead as if the media is what it is, a representative and extension of the fans; they were gracious about and toward each other . . . I cheered their friendly competition, and so did much of the country. . . . All in all it was great fun watching them. We were quite lucky in our choice of contestants. Imagine, said my colleague Roger Angell of the *New Yorker*, if it had been Albert Belle and Barry Bonds.[15]

In fact, it is extremely unfair to lump Albert Belle and Barry Bonds together. Belle had on more than one occasion been accused of violently attacking and making obscene gestures at fans. There is no evidence that Bonds has ever done anything of this nature. Both Belle and Bonds, however, have fulfilled a similar stereotypical role for baseball writers, one that resonates with a long tradition of representing a particular kind of black male as uncontrolled and violent (see discussion in Chapter 5). When writing about the McGwire–Sosa home-run race, Halberstam states that he did "not pick up" any racial bias in favor of McGwire. Perhaps not, but the connection that Angel and Halberstam draw between Belle and Bonds suggests that race is still powerfully meaningful and have played an important role in the way that reporters for national media outlets have framed their understanding of Barry Bonds.

Local coverage of Bonds in San Francisco has not always been kind, but it has also shown his career from multiple perspectives. For example, in January 2000, the *San Francisco Examiner* ran a story about Bonds paying a visit to a 102-year-old Polish immigrant named Anna Payne. Bonds' mother had read an article in the *Examiner* about Payne in a feature profiling five different centenarians and had called her son and told him to read it. Payne had mentioned that it was a dream of hers to meet Barry Bonds, having been a devoted fan of his and of Bobby's. The article details how Bonds went to her home in the modest outer Mission district of San Francisco and spent the afternoon laughing and talking to his new friend. He arranged for Payne to attend a game during the opening week of Pac Bell Park and to visit the locker room and meet Hall of Fame outfielder Willie Mays, manager Dusty Baker, and his father, Bobby. The article's author Julian Guthrie writes that Bonds

> wanted an intimate gathering, objecting to media presence. He finally agreed to allow a reporter to attend, but insisted on no photos. By the end of the visit, after Payne and Bonds had hugged, kissed and discovered they were soul mates, Bonds gave the OK for a reporter's photos to be published. Contrary to his sometimes surly image, Bonds was candid, affectionate and loving with Payne. He signed a bat and ball for her and said, "Whenever you need me, you call me. If you get sick or anything before the opening games in April, I will fly you to spring training."[16]

This story was not widely reported. Unlike the more unflattering details of his divorce proceedings or an unsubstantiated paternity suit by a former pornographic film star who had connections to O. J. Simpson, it was not picked up by wire services and distributed nationally. In part, this is probably due to Bonds' own insistence that the visit not be turned into a media event. However, it also does not fit into the mold that had been cast for Bonds, one that would later allow Reilly and Halberstam to characterize him as seamlessly bad. Many who have known Bonds, such as former teammate Todd Benzinger, agree with Reilly and Halberstam that Bonds can be rude and disagreeable, but they also point out that he is a complex person. In a letter to *Sports Illustrated* written in response to Reilly's piece, Benzinger wrote that he remembered Barry Bonds, "picking up huge checks at restaurants; embarrassing a magician at a team party by yelling out the secret to every trick he had; getting down on his hands and knees and playing with my then four-year-old daughter at a kid's birthday party and telling me, 'she's the cutest little girl I've ever seen in my life!'"[17] As Bonds approached McGwire's record, this more complex image was one that few in the national media seemed ready to embrace.

Bonds continued his march toward McGwire's record. One of his most stunning performances came on September 9 in an extra-inning victory over the Colorado Rockies. Bonds entered the game with 60 home runs and left the extra-inning victory with 63. After the game, even Jeff Kent expressed nothing but encouragement toward Bonds. He told reporters, " 'I get criticized for not running up there and giving him a big bear hug after his home runs. But it's his time. He likes that. It's always neat to hit behind him. To watch him work pitchers and take good swings and be patient. It's been pretty incredible to watch this year."[18]

Following the Colorado series, the Giants had traveled to Houston to play against the Astros. Anticipation surrounding the game was high. Houston's Enron Field, named after the soon-to-be-deposed energy corporation, was known as one of the best home-run parks in the game. On September 10, an officer from the Houston police department, along with manager Dusty Baker, Brian Sabean, and assistant general manager Ned Colletti, went to Bonds' hotel room to inform him that a threat had been made upon his life. A caller had phoned a local television station and left a message stating that he was going to gun-down Bonds.

Of course, Bonds would never have to worry about taking the field the next day. On September 11, terrorists hijacked four planes, crashing two into the twin towers of New York's World Trade Center and a third into the Pentagon Building. A final plane went down in a field in west-central Pennsylvania, apparently forced down before it managed to reach its target. Baseball games were canceled, and Bonds' assault upon McGwire's record was no longer on the front page. In his first comments after the tragedy, Bonds said, "We have to move on eventually, but it just seems too early right now. . . . I just feel for those people. Innocent people are gone. It's devastating. It's just not right."[19]

When the season resumed, Bonds continued on his streak, albeit with a somewhat less enthusiastic sense of celebration. When the Giants returned to Houston in early October for the make-up series, Bonds had 69, one home run away from tying McGwire. Anticipation among many baseball fans was high, yet outside of the San Francisco Bay Area, attention to the record was relatively understated. CBS reporter John Blackstone called the reaction to Bonds' home-run chase "understandably muted" in the wake of the tragedies of September 11 and notes that Bonds, "aloof with teammates, unavailable and unfriendly to the media," had become "kinder, gentler."[20]

In Houston, Astros manager Larry Dierker seemed intent upon not allowing Bonds to break the record on their home field. In fact, according to Suchon's count in the middle of the last game of the series against the Astros, 51 of the last 64 pitches thrown to Bonds were balls. Despite his lack of selection, Bonds finally connected in the ninth inning of the last game of the series, a 454-foot blastoff of Wilfredo Rodriguez.

The Giants were returning to San Francisco to play the Dodgers for the last series of the season. Not only was Bonds on the verge of hitting 71 home runs, but the team was hot on the heals of the Arizona Diamondbacks for the National League West title. On October 5, Bonds faced Dodgers pitcher Chan Ho

Park in the bottom of the first in a game that the Giants needed to win to stay alive in the playoff race. Losing by the score of 5–0, Bonds hit a 1–0 delivery 421 feet over the right center field wall. In the third, with the Giants now losing 8–4, Bonds delivered again, knocking out number 72 once again off a pitch by Park. The Giants continued to rally, with shortstop Rich Aurilia hitting a home run in the sixth that tied the game at 10. In the top of the seventh, however, the Dodgers scored once more. It proved to be the decisive run, and the Giants had lost.

The game had lasted 4 hours and 27 minutes. It was 12:30 in the morning. The Giants had lost the longest nine-inning game in major league history, and they had been eliminated from playoff contention. It was an odd time to celebrate. Filled with emotion, Bonds told the crowd, most of whom had stayed until the very end, "To my teammates, we worked real hard, and we're going to work real hard again. I love you all very much. It's an honor to play with a bunch of guys like this behind me. I'll play for you any time, any day of the week, any hour, any year."[21] Fans chanted, "Sign him!" and "Four more years!" Teammate Shawn Dunston, who earlier in the season had bet Bonds that he would break McGwire's record, stepped to the microphone and told the crowd, "I want to thank everybody for coming out and supporting the Giants. Barry really loves you, and he really does want to come back Peter."

On CNN, Ken Rosenthal of the *New York Times* noted the remarkable achievement that Bonds had made during the season, noting not only that he had broken an amazing home-run record but that "he's going to set the National League slugger percentage record by almost—or more than a 100 points. He's going to set the All-Time slugger percentage record. He's got the All-Time Walks record. Home run frequency, all of these things, he's accomplishing. Just a tremendous season, a historic season for Barry Bonds." When asked what Bonds' home-run chase had done "for America" at a time of crisis, Rosenthal responded that it was an important diversion, which is what sports "should be."[22]

As much as Bonds' home-run chase had provided a diversion, it was upstaged, in many respects, by the final games for two major league legends, Tony Gwynn and Cal Ripkin Jr. Ripkin's game was a gala affair, nationally televised and attended by the commissioner of baseball and former president Bill Clinton. Credited with bringing a wholesome image back to baseball after the crippling strike of 1994, Ripkin was connected to a story that was a no less uncomplicated antithesis to the one attached to Bonds. One must wonder if the celebration would have been so muted if he had been the one to have broken McGwire's record in the wake of September 11.

On the last day of the season, Bonds hit his 73rd home run, and that fall, the Giants signed him to a five-year contract extension. The contract was settled when both sides agreed to go to arbitration. For the Giants, it meant a decision to stay with Bonds over Jeff Kent, and for Bonds it meant a long term commitment to a team without a recent tradition of winning. Worth $90 million, Bonds was certain not to ever live in poverty, but he still might never live to play in a World Series game.

NOTES

1. J. Pearlman, "Appreciating Bonds," *Sports Illustrated*, June 5, 2000, 48–50, 53.

2. William Ladson, "The Complete Player," *Sporting News*, July 12, 1999, 12.

3. Josh Suchon, interview with author, May 15, 2003.

4. Chuck Johnson, "Bonds-Mays Ties Go Deep," *USA Today*, September 2, 2003, 1C.

5. Suchon, *This Gracious Season*, 72–73.

6. Ibid., 46–47.

7. Ibid., 59.

8. Ibid.

9. Ibid., 89.

10. Hal Bodley, "Charming Superstar or Selfish Malcontent? It's Up to Bonds," *USA Today*, July 11, 2001, 4C.

11. "Ray Ratto Discusses Barry Bonds' Public Relations Persona," *All Things Considered*, National Public Radio, August 29, 2001.

12. David Halberstam, "Why America Will Never Love Barry Bonds," ESPN.Com Page Two, http://espn.go.com/page2/s/halberstam/010719.html.

13. Rick Reilly, "Life of Reilly," *Sports Illustrated*, August 27, 2001, 102.

14. Suchon, *This Gracious Season*, 250.

15. Halberstam, "Why America Will Never Love Barry Bonds," http://espn.go.com/page2/s/halberstam/010719.html.

16. Julian Guthrie, "Barry Bonds Visits with Fan, 102," *San Francisco Examiner*, January 15, 2000.

17. Quoted in Suchon, *This Gracious Season*, 338.

18. Ibid., 290–291.

19. Ibid., 295–296.

20. John Blackstone, "For the Books; Meaning behind Barry Bonds and His Struggle to Break a Home Run Record," *Sunday Morning* (CBS Telecast), September 30, 2001.

21. Henry Schulman, "A Day of Mixed Emotions," *San Francisco Chronicle*, October 7, 2001.

22. Kyra Phillips, "Barry Bonds Hits 72nd Home-Run of the Season," *CNN Saturday Morning News* (Telecast), October 6, 2001.

Barry Bonds greets teammate Jeff Kent at home plate after Kent's third-inning home run in Game 2 of the 2002 World Series between the Giants and the Anaheim Angels. Despite complimenting each other as hitters in the San Francisco line-up, Bonds and Kent did not get along well off the field. © *San Francisco Chronicle/CORBIS SABA.*

A DREAM COME TRUE . . .
ALMOST, 2002

Perhaps it was fitting that Barry Bonds' 73rd home run should land in the out-field stands rather than in the waters of McCovey Cove. If it had sailed into the bay, it is likely that a singular fan would have been able to paddle to the ball before all of the rest. There might not have been an ounce of controversy to dis-tract anybody from the achievement itself. Instead, the object landed in a crowd, ultimately becoming locked in a battle between two litigious fans, Alex Popov and Patrick Hayashi. Popov initially caught the ball and dropped it after excited fans mobbed him. Hayashi became the beneficiary of this chaos, picking up the loose ball. After the game, Popov filed suit against Hayashi, a suit that was ul-timately settled when a San Francisco Superior Court judge ordered the ball to be auctioned to the highest bidder and for the two litigants to evenly share the proceeds.[1]

Just as Bonds' home-run ball was locked in controversy, Bonds' home-run season ended on a bittersweet note. Not only had his performance during the season not been enough to get the Giants into the playoffs, but his unresolved contract made his future with the team look uncertain. On November 19, 2001, Barry Bonds learned that he had won his fourth National League Most Valu-able Player award. Bonds had now won more MVP trophies than any player in the history of Major League Baseball, but Bonds expressed a sense of emptiness that reflected his uncertain status.

"It was fun," he told reporters after learning that he had won the award. "I wish we would have went to the World Series. It would've been a lot funner." When reporters talked to him about his remarkable season, he replied, "The most important thing for me is winning. I really want an opportunity to win. I've played a long time. And I really want to win."[2]

At the time that he was being celebrated as the best player of the 2001 season in the National League, Bonds was also testing the free agent waters, seeing if there were, perhaps, a winning team that was interested in his services and that could pay his salary. Many in baseball expected the New York Yankees to end up with Bonds. Others speculated that he would go to the Mets or even the Dodgers. As Bonds' agent Scott Boras and the Giants management negotiated over a contract that would keep him in a Giants uniform, both Bonds and the San Francisco front office maintained at least a public expression of a desire to come to an agreement. Giants president Peter McGowan told reporters, "It's good for the organization when the person considered to be the best player in the game is playing for you. I think the year that he had was as great a year as any player ever had. I think he's going to accomplish a lot more."

Bonds replied in kind, stating that, more than money, he wanted an organization to demonstrate that they appreciated his talents. "I just want to feel wanted," said Bonds, "and I think that's the key of any baseball player. You just want to feel your team is behind you and supportive of you." Bonds added that he wanted to finish his career in San Francisco but was willing to go elsewhere if offered a better package. "It's a perfect story. You're raised in a city and you win in that city. But sometimes it doesn't work out that way."[3]

The Giants made an early effort to show that they "wanted" their top performer to stay. They made an offer on the last day of November and another one reportedly worth $72 million over four years on December 13. Within a week, Bonds agreed to salary arbitration with the Giants. This meant that he could not negotiate with any other team and that he was committed to playing another year in San Francisco. According to Suchon, the Giants were the only team that anyone can verify had made an offer to Bonds. "No other team ever publicly acknowledged making a contract offer to the greatest player of his generation, coming off the greatest offensive season in baseball history, whose goal is to play another five years in pursuit of the most storied career records in baseball history, everything from 3,000 hits to 755 homers."[4] In mid-January, Bonds and the Giants came to an agreement, with Bonds accepting a five-year contract worth roughly $18 million a year in base salary, signing bonuses, and deferred payments through 2011. The structure of Bonds' contract allowed Magowan to stay close to his payroll budget and keep the player who he hoped would take his team to its first World Series championship in San Francisco. Working out before the 2002 season, Bonds told Suchon, "Everybody knows my main goal is winning a World Series. Whatever it takes, I'm willing to do it."[5]

In 2002, Bonds put in a performance that matched his words. Bonds' .370

batting average was enough for him to win the first batting title of his career. Even more impressively, combined with his record 198 walks, Bonds set a major league record for on-base percentage with a .582 average. The old mark of .551 was set by Ted Williams and had stood for sixty-one years. Even though his home-run total "dropped" to 46, and his .799 slugging percentage was not quite as good as in the previous year, many considered his 2002 performance the best ever. It was good enough to get the Giants into the playoffs and to earn him his fifth career National League Most Valuable Player award. Combined with Jeff Kent's award in 2000, the Giants had earned three consecutive MVP awards. The only other single team to dominate the award in such a fashion during the previous fifty years had been the Cincinnati Reds with Joe Morgan in 1975–1976 and George Foster in 1977.[6]

Despite their success together for the benefit of the team, Kent and Bonds continued to exhibit a cold relationship on and off the field. In fact, the conflict turned heated early in the season when the Giants were struggling, trailing the rival Dodgers for the division lead. Bonds, in fact, had expressed a sense of alienation from the entire team, complaining publicly that his pitchers were not challenging opposing line-ups enough after he had been brushed back from the plate. A few weeks later, manager Dusty Baker had insulted Kent by stating that he was disturbed by the number of times that Bonds had been walked by opposing teams but surprised at the number of times that this strategy had worked. In mid-June while playing in a series against the San Diego Padres, the conflict between Bonds and Kent erupted into an open fight in the dugout. Reportedly, Kent criticized a play by third baseman David Bell, and Bonds came to Bell's defense. Eventually, Bonds put his hand on Kent's neck and pushed him against the wall of the dugout, and the two had to be physically separated.[7]

The conflict between Bonds and Kent, of course, was not anything new by the 2002 season, having been aired during the previous season during the infamous Reilly column in *Sports Illustrated*. It had become even more intense, reportedly, after the Giants signed Bonds to the multiyear contract, which left little room for Kent's salary in the Giants long-term budget. Furthermore, after winning the MVP award in 2000, Kent had been significantly outperformed by Bonds.

For many sportswriters and fans, however, the conflict between the two became more than simply one between players; it was also between symbols of particular types of people, types that have, as previously discussed, racial overtones grounded in a history of racial representation. Bonds has been portrayed within a particular kind of African American stereotype that highlights perceived dangers of black manhood and leadership through images of violence, indifference to white authority, and laziness. Kent also conveyed a stereotype, one of a white working-class male "red neck" who was hardworking and dedicated, yet abrasive and unrefined. As much as Bonds and Kent might have had a real feud, they also had a symbolic conflict that resonated with sportswriters and fans. We see this in the reporting of Reilly, as well as in that of other syndicated sports columnists. For example, after the Bonds–Kent blowup in San Diego, Ross Newhan of the *Los Angeles Times* wrote the following words about the two in a column that appeared in papers around the United States, such as the *Milwaukee Journal Sentinel.*

> Bonds, the Bay Area-born son of former Giant star Bobby Bonds and godson of Giant Hall of Famer Willie Mays, and Kent, the blue-collar Texas rancher, have kept their respectful distance, neither friends nor particularly friendly, for five years. . . . It is Bonds' team, and no matter what the hard-nosed Kent thinks about the left fielder's poses after his long and frequent home runs, his failure to run all out on some ground balls and base hits, the elbow padding he's allowed to wear when batting, the time off he gets when games become routs and the in-your-face schedule he's allowed to keep, nothing will change that.[8]

Writing from Los Angeles, Newhan's column actually focused mostly upon the hope that the Bonds–Kent fight would help the Dodgers win the division. However, it is important to pay attention to the adjectives and descriptive phrases that the columnist provides in a shorthand fashion, ones that serve as a kind of code for readers. These codes transform a conflict between two players on a baseball team into a cultural battle between two "types" of people, one with social significance beyond the pennant race. Newhan describes Kent as "blue-collar" and "hard-nosed," and even links him to the image of a cowboy by labeling Kent a "Texas rancher" (even though Kent actually grew up in suburban Orange County, California, and bought his ranch only after becoming a highly paid Major League Baseball player). By contrast, Bonds is presented less as a hard worker who earned his greatness on the field and more as a player who inherited his talents, born with a proverbial silver baseball glove on his hand (the son and godson of baseball greats). He shows off ("poses" after home runs), exhibits laziness (fails to "run all out" for grounders and hits), and is cowardly (wears elbow padding) and obnoxious (keeps an "in-your-face schedule" . . . what that actually means is not clear in the column).

Shortly after the fight in San Diego, manager Dusty Baker switched Bonds and Kent in the line-up, batting Kent ahead of Bonds. The strategy seemed to work, and Kent began performing as he had in 2000. With the Giants trailing the Arizona Diamondbacks during the month by as many as twelve games, sports columnist Ray Ratto of the *San Francisco Chronicle* focused upon the MVP race between Bonds and Kent, finding that the most compelling story coming out of the Giants clubhouse. He once again provides a picture of Bonds as alienated from his teammates and of Kent as the more popular of the two. Recalling the 2000 MVP race, he notes that Giants players supported Kent and that sportswriters voted for Kent, in numbers that did not match the teammates' statistical performances. Ratto writes that when sportswriters surveyed Giants players,

> The results of the polling were remarkable. Well, interesting, anyway. Asked the question, "Who's more valuable to your team, Kent or Bonds?" almost every player and coach said Kent. A few demurred, but only Ellis Burks [an African American player] said Bonds without out qualification. Which is fine, except that the statistics were not so disparate that the final voting (Kent finished with 22 first-place votes, Bonds six despite Bonds hitting more home runs and driving in as many runs) should have been so lopsided. Kent had an MVP season by any standard, so the result wasn't questioned, only the margin of victory. The support for Kent within his own clubhouse was the clear difference in explaining that margin.[9]

The public image and personality profile that Ratto argues cost Bonds so many votes in his 2000 MVP is very similar to the one that Reilly describes in his "24 against 1" *Sports Illustrated* column. In fact, Ratto was probably correct. Had Bonds and Kent had equivalent seasons in 2002, Kent would have likely been voted MVP once more. During the middle of the 2002 season, it not only looked as if this might happen but also looked as if the MVP might be the biggest prize available for either player. The general bargaining agreement between the Major League Players Association and Major League Baseball had expired, and as in 1994, the two organizations were deadlocked in negotiations. It looked for certain as if a strike were unavoidable. Given the negative sentiments generated by the past strike, both sides seemed more determined this time to come to an agreement. Yet having had his bad image cast to a large degree during the past work stoppage, Bonds certainly did not help his image when he was quoted as saying that if baseball went on strike, "It's entertainment. It will come back. A lot of companies go on strike. . . . And people still ride the bus."[10]

In fact, the players and owners did come to an agreement and avoided a strike. As they did so, Bonds was also in the process of avoiding any doubt that he, not Jeff Kent, was the National League's Most Valuable Player. On August 9 against the Pirates, he hit his 600th career home run off pitcher Kip Wells, a shot that was estimated to have traveled 421 feet. By the end of the season, Bonds was not only the clear choice for MVP but had led his team to 95 wins, 2½ games behind the division-leading Arizona Diamondbacks, but good enough to win the National League Wild Card spot in the playoffs.

Bonds' stellar performances in 2001 and 2002 also led to a set of rumors to swirl about him that once more threatened to detract from his accomplishments. Sportswriters, television commentators, and fans all began to discuss whether or not Bonds was taking illegal performance-enhancing steroids. Even though they had only anecdotal evidence for making such allegations beyond the visible transformations in Bonds' build since he first broke into baseball, reporters in the press box began to circulate gossip about Bonds' ability to hit with a new level of power so late in his career.

These rumors became more pronounced toward the end of May, when infielder Ken Caminiti alleged in *Sports Illustrated* that half of all Major League Baseball players take steroids to improve their performance. About a week after this cover story appeared in the magazine, Caminiti appeared on ESPN and downplayed his earlier estimate, but he had already said enough for many fans to feel that their suspicions, first heightened during the famous battle between Sosa and McGwire for the home-run record in 1998, were true.

In fact, once fans got over the euphoria of the 1998 season, the famous home-run barrage highlighted just how inflated this statistic was becoming in Major League Baseball. The total number of home runs hit by the home-run champion of each league between 1984 and 1993 was 838. Between 1994 and 2003, this number jumped to 1,038, and that's after a strike that cut the 1994 season short by nearly two months. In the earlier ten-season span, only one player hit over 50 home runs in either league (Cecil Fielder with 51 for Detroit in 1990). During the second ten-year span, a home-run champion in one league or the other hit over 50 home runs ten times. In fact, in 1998 and 1999, Sammy Sosa hit over 60 home runs each season and never even won a home-run title! Some speculated that these high home-run totals were due to a "juiced ball," that is, a baseball that carried a little bit of an extra bounce, while others wondered whether the new ballparks around the league were more home-run-friendly. Caminiti's comments raised speculation, already hot, that the frequency with which baseballs were being hit over fences might have something to do with performance-enhancing drugs.

Even before the season had begun, sports columnist Allan Berra, writing for Salon.com, unintentionally stoked the rumor flames by noting the oddity of how Bonds' best seasons have come at the end of his career. In an article actually meant as an expression of admiration for Bonds' performances, Barra wrote,

> All through the second half of last season, I flogged the sports press for not giving Barry Bonds enough credit for his incredible season, the greatest in National League and quite possibly in Major League history. (On paper, the only season in baseball history that equals it is Babe Ruth's 1924 season.) But something was wrong with what Bonds did in 2001. I confess that I don't have a firm idea as to what it was, but *something* was wrong. By wrong, I'm not making a moral judgment; I mean that something was out of whack in the universe. For at least the last 15 seasons, Bonds has been the best player in baseball. That is not the issue. The issue is that Bonds turned 37 last July, and in no previous season had he ever hit so many as 50 home runs. In fact, in his entire career he only exceeded 42 home runs twice. In 15 previous major league seasons, Bonds had averaged 33 home runs per year, and then, all of a sudden, at an age when nearly every ballplayer experiences a sharp drop-off, he increased his average production by 221 percent. Why? How?[11]

Barra actually speculates that the specially made maplewood bat that Bonds uses may have helped to increase his home-run production, and his article is more about what the increase in home runs and strikeouts was doing to the experience of watching a baseball game, yet many interpreted his words as an implied accusation that Bonds could have hit 73 home runs only if he were on steroids. He acknowledged that his column had been understood this way in October but asserted that this had been a misinterpretation.

> I may have given the wrong impression earlier this year when I mentioned [Bonds' elevated game after the age of 36] in connection with steroid use in baseball. I wasn't implying that Bonds was using steroids. I was suggesting very strongly that if steroids are not studied, and if the study warrants, banned, the fans would soon begin to suspect the integrity of baseball statistics—and then, inevitably, that of the game itself. If Barry Bonds' incredible three-season binge is due to steroids, then it would stand to reason that some other player would have similar numbers or at least have increased his earlier numbers along the same percentages that Bonds has. Nobody has, so I'll leave off the steroid discussion for now.[12]

It is revealing, however, that so many readers and fellow sportswriters interpreted Barra's column to have been about steroids, despite the author's strong expressions of admiration for Bonds. Part of this may be due to the factors that are larger than Bonds himself. Drug scandals that have affected nearly every sport have made many in the general public distrustful of fantastic athletic achievements and new athletic records, whether the player is or is not generally liked (as with Mark McGwire) or generally disliked (as with Barry Bonds).

At the same time, as allegations of steroid use in baseball began to emerge, many reporters and fans were suspicious that Bonds was a guilty party. A local reporter told freelance reporter David Grann, " 'The running bet in the office is that Barry's head has grown,' which is a sign of steroids."[13] Grann, who spent a great deal of time with Bonds, was not party to any steroid use that might have been taking place, yet he did witness aspects of Bonds' behavior that also *might* explain his outstanding performance late in his career. Grann observed that Bonds "often gets up at 5 in the morning and runs sprints, even after night games. He lifts every day, isolating one segment of his body—his shoulders or calves or abdomen. . . . To stay in condition he eats six specially prepared meals a day, consisting of fish, chicken, turkey, vegetables or, on rare instances, beef; each meal has 350 to 450 calories." Bonds has his blood tested every month to make sure that he has the right levels of minerals in his system. In 2002, he bragged about having the lowest body fat of anyone on the team at spring training.[14]

Bonds may or may not, in fact, be on steroids, yet the focus upon this possibility over the work that he puts into staying fit has the effect of diminishing the degree to which the improvement in his performance is due to the work he has put into his career. Over the next year, he would not be able to shake interest in whether he was using performance-enhancing drugs, but in 2002, Bonds was able to break free from his reputation as a player who could not perform well in the playoffs. In opening best-of-five Divisional Series, Bonds was finally able to avenge his earlier playoff losses against the Atlanta Braves as a member of the Pittsburgh Pirates. Down two games to one, the Giants rallied to beat Atlanta at home to tie the Series, and then win Game 5 in front of the Braves home fans. Bonds hit three home runs in the Series and hit .294. Against St. Louis in the NLCS, Bonds hit another home run, and the Giants routed the Cardinals four games to one. The normally reserved Bonds led the charge out of the dugout when Kenny Lofton hit his game-winning single to give the Giants the National League pennant and send them to the World Series.

Bonds had long said that his ultimate goal was just to make it to the World Series, and he had finally achieved it. Against the Anaheim Angels, he performed as if a weight had been lifted off his shoulders. Despite being walked 13 times in the seven-game Series, he still managed to hit 4 home runs and 2 doubles. For the Series, he hit 471, with 6 of his 8 hits for extra bases, amounting to a 1.294 slugging percentage. When his hitting numbers are added to his walks, Bonds had a .700 on-base percentage. In other words, in a sport where reaching base 4 out of every 10 times at bat is considered successful, Bonds did so 7 out of every 10 times during the World Series.

Had he Giants won the series, Bonds would have been named Most Valuable Player without question. However, things did not work out so well for San Francisco. After splitting the opening two games in Anaheim, the Giants won two of three at home, the last game by the score of 16 to 4. Even though the series was heading back to Southern California, it looked as if the Giants had the momentum to win, leading three games to two, and for 6½ innings in Game 6, San Francisco did nothing to disappoint their fans.

After four innings without a score, the Giants got on the board with three in the fifth, a fourth in the sixth on a solo homer by Bonds, and one more in the seventh. Then disaster struck for San Francisco. The Angels scored three in the bottom of the seventh, and with no outs and a runner on first in the bottom of the eighth, Darin Erstad homered to make it a 5-to-4 game. Tim Salmon then singled off Tim Worrell and was sent off for pinch runner Chone Figgens. This sent Garret Anderson, representing the go-ahead run, to the plate. He connected for a bloop hit that Bonds misplayed, allowing him to end up on second base. Troy Glaus followed by doubling against the left field wall over Bonds' head, scoring Anderson. It was all the Angels would need. After losing in such a heartbreaking fashion, the Giants then fell meekly in Game 7 by the score of 4 to 1, and the Angels celebrated their first-ever World Series title. The series MVP was Troy Glaus.

Bonds, frustrated by his team's collapse and by his own role in it, showed his emotions to reporters in the locker room after the game. As reporters crowded around him and pressed against his son Nikolai, Bonds glared back in an image that was caught by a television camera operator and growled, "Back off or I'll snap!" This scene of a vanquished Bonds provided his critics with all of the material that they needed. Reilly and Halberstam each wrote columns that once more took a critical look at Bonds.

Reilly headlined his column after Bonds' infamous "Back off or I'll snap!" line. He wrote,

> Don't you feel a little sorry for Barry Bonds? True, Bonds has the warmth of a dyspeptic IRS auditor. He dispenses more snarls than twin Dobermans. He's rude, insular and grouchy. And that's on his birthday. But nobody, not even Barry Bonds, deserves a World Series week like he just had. All his life he'd dreamed of getting to one of these babies, and when he did it brought him all the joy of an upper G.I. cleansing.

Reilly not only expressed gleeful sarcasm over Bonds' loss but even suggested, albeit tounge-in-cheek, that the team may have intentionally thrown the series to get back at their hated teammate.

> Hell, maybe it was his teammates' revenge. After all, in the postseason he'd treated them like strangers on a prison bus. When they whipped the St. Louis Cardinals for the National League pennant, no champagne sprayed him. And during the World Series Game 3 introductions, he was the only player on the Giants to jog straight to his spot without greeting the line of teammates. . . . Suddenly, it seemed, they were paying back their cleanup hitter. In the No. 3 slot, second baseman Jeff Kent had one big game out of seven. The No. 5 hitter, human sar-pei Benito Santiago, seemed to need an Anaheimlich maneuver. Two guys, Rich Aurelia and Reggie Sanders, struck out nine times each.[15]

Reilly was probably only kidding when he suggested that the rest of the Giants may have tanked the series to get back at their moody left fielder, yet his humor is symptomatic of the manner in which Bonds' critics have long treated him. If Bonds had only one good game out of seven, Reilly might have cast him as, once more, the great choker, a player with tremendous talents but lacking the character to lead his team to victory when it really counts. For Kent, however, underperformance becomes revenge against his "rude," "insular," and "grouchy" teammate.

Halberstam, in a more serious—and in many ways more bitter—criticism of Bonds, also felt his past column had been vindicated by the Giants loss, particularly after Bonds told reporters after Game 6 to quit their jobs and find another line of work. Halberstam notes, "I like that, telling them to find other work—it really sums up his value system, and what he's about, and it shows that he understands what they do, all the free coverage they give baseball, day in and day out, has nothing to do with the size of his paycheck." He goes on to repeat his feeling that Bonds is abusive in his treatment of reporters. Recounting his own experiences covering Vietnam, the violent civil rights battle in the South, and the assassinations of Robert Kennedy and Martin Luther King, Halberstam notes that reporters have a job that is more important, and pays less, than that of a star baseball player, yet his most stinging critique is more about the attitude that he feels Bonds displays toward the game of baseball.

> What I really think is so unfortunate about all of this is that it should be fun to cheer for him, someone playing so well so late in his career, but it isn't. Even more, it doesn't look like there's very much

fun in it for him. I've watched closely over the last year, and in sharp contrast to Mark McGwire and Sammy Sosa in their hour of fame, for instance, I don't think it's a cumulative portrait of a man having a very good time. Brilliant at what he does, yes, but enjoying it . . . I don't think so.[16]

Other sports reporters have echoed Halberstam's claim that Bonds plays the game without a sense of joy, but for others, this particular criticism is particularly unfair. Many who covered Mark McGwire, for example, note that he was under tremendous stress the year that he hit 70 home runs and did not always exhibit a sense of joy when confronted by reporters after games. In fact, McGwire enjoyed the public spotlight so much he retired just two years after his second consecutive season with more than 60 home runs, isolating himself and refusing to do interviews with reporters. *San Francisco Chronicle* sports columnist David Steele feels that this criticism reflects an unreasonable expectation on the part of many fans and a lack of respect for the ways that Bonds does perform.

He throws himself into it. He shows up in great shape and does all the things to improve himself every year, and that's probably why he's still playing at this level now. Yet he's never come across—and people write this all the time—"Oh, he doesn't look like he's enjoying it. Why can't you enjoy it . . ." And it becomes a criticism. You know, you're not having enough fun doing this. You're not having enough fun for *me*. You're not showing *me* how much you love this grand old game. . . . You hear and see stuff like that and it makes you think, okay, are you guys looking for a reason to just get on him? I mean, that's really kind of a reach. In reality, what difference does it make?[17]

Despite having lost in the World Series, 2002 was a high point for Bonds. He had followed his spectacular 2001 season with an even more impressive one in 2002 and was for the first time the unanimous choice for league MVP, winning it for a record fifth time in his career. He had finally achieved one of his major goals by making it to, and nearly winning, the World Series, and he had not only performed well in the postseason but almost single-handedly carried his team through to Game 7. In 2003, he would once again put in a stellar performance and set new milestones. However, in the off-season, Dusty Baker, long at odds with the Giants ownership, would decline an offer to return to the team and instead take a post as manager of the Chicago Cubs. Under the management of a great former Giant, Felipe Alou, Bonds once again led the Giants to the postseason, but he did so facing the greatest and most tragic loss of his life.

NOTES

1. "Owner of Bonds' Historic Home Run Ball Headed toward Trial," Associated Press, November 26, 2001; Gwen Knapp, "Bonds' No. 73 Sets No Records at Auction," *San Francisco Chronicle*, June 26, 2003.

2. Rafael Hermoso, "Bonds Is Voted MVP a Record Fourth Time," *New York Times*, November 20, 2001, S4.

3. Henry Schulman, "Bonds in Limelight," *San Francisco Chronicle*, November 20, 2001, C1.

4. Josh Suchon, *This Gracious Season,* 387.

5. Ibid., 390.

6. Mark Camps, "S.F. Equals Cincinnati's MVP Feat," *San Francisco Chronicle*, November 27, 2002, C2.

7. Ross Newhan, "There Are No Winners When It Comes to Bonds–Kent Feud," *Milwaukee Journal Sentinel*, June 30, 2002, 5C.

8. Ibid.

9. Ray Ratto, "Another Kent–Bonds Scrap—for MVP," *San Francisco Chronicle*, August 16, 2002, C1.

10. Quoted in Grann, "Baseball without Metaphor."

11. Allen Barra, "What Barry Bonds Did Wrong," Salon.com, March 28, 2002, www.salon.com/news/sports/col/berra/2002/03/28/bonds.

12. Allen Barra, "Barry and the Babe," Salon.com, October 25, 2002, http://archive.salon.com/news/sports/col/barra/2002/10/25/bonds/.

13. Grann, "Baseball without Metaphor."

14. Ibid.

15. Rick Reilly, "Back Off or I'll Snap," *Sports Illustrated*, November 4, 2002, 96.

16. David Halberstam, "Are You Having Fun Yet, Barry?" ESPN.com, Page 2, October 29, 2002, http://espn.go.com/page2/s/halberstam/021029.html.

17. David Steele, interview with author, February 27, 2002.

8

PRIVATE STRUGGLES AND PUBLIC IMAGES, 2003

When Barry Bonds arrived for spring training in February 2003, he admitted that he was finally feeling the effects of the aging process. "It's like my dad said, I'm still faster than you, but just once. If you want to race me, I'll beat you, but I need a whole day to recover."[1] In addition, he still felt the sting of the previous season's heartbreaking World Series loss to the Angels, yet he was able to put the defeat behind him, and he credited his wife, Liz, for helping him do it. "My wife woke me up to reality. I got my wish to be in a World Series and it was over with. No what-ifs, no worries, no nothing. She always looks to me for answers. She gave me the answer I didn't know about. You got your wish. You wanted to be in a World Series. Now cut it loose. It's been gone ever since."[2] Bonds vowed never again to wish only to go to the World Series, but instead to win it.

In spring training it looked as if Bonds' biggest worries were his aching legs, some minor elbow surgery, and getting back to the fall classic. However, soon after the season started, it was clear that the Giants pennant chase was of secondary importance. Barry's father, Bobby, already having battled lung cancer for about a year, needed surgery to remove a malignant tumor from his brain. As the season progressed, Bobby's health continued to degenerate, requiring Barry to take time off to help care for him. Despite the strain created by his father's health problems, Bonds continued to play, and his focus seemed to become only more intense. With Jeff Kent gone and Felipe Alou the team's new manager, many had doubts as to whether Bonds could lead his team back to another postseason birth, yet as the season progressed, it was clear that Bonds was still a force hitting behind just about anybody.

Barry Bonds hugs his father, Bobby Bonds, after hitting his 500th career home run on April 18, 2001, in the eighth inning of a game against the Los Angeles Dodgers in San Francisco. Bobby Bonds' death in August 2003 deeply affected his son, except on the field, where Barry continued to excel despite his concern over his father's failing health. © *Reuters/CORBIS*.

The Giants began the season in first place and, despite stumbling into a tie a few times during the season, never relinquished their lead. In addition to leading his team back to the playoffs, Bonds set one of the most impressive career milestones in June, when he became the first player in major league history to steal 500 bases while also hitting over 500 home runs. Against the Dodgers nearly unstoppable closer Eric Gagne, Bonds came up to bat in an extra-inning game between two teams tied for the division lead. Gagne walked Bonds on a 3–2 pitch, and Bonds then stole second base uncontested to set the record. Accused in the past of stealing bases unnecessarily to pad his own statistics, Bonds' 500th steal was a brilliant strategic move that put him in scoring position with no outs. Two batters later, Benito Santiago singled to left, and Bonds scored to give his team the victory. Alou praised his star after the game, saying, "In that last at-bat, he was dominant without hitting a home run. I hope people don't judge Barry only by the home runs he hits. He's a supreme player."[3]

Of all Bonds' achievements as a baseball player, his 500/500 mark may be the most difficult for another player to overtake. Vladimir Guerrero and Alex Rodriguez are the two contemporary players who have a chance, but no other player in major league history has even managed to steal 400 bases while hitting over 400 home runs. It should be no surprise that the two who have come closest to doing so were Bonds' godfather, Willie Mays (338 steals and 660 home runs), and his father, Bobby Bonds (461 steals and 332 homers).[4]

Bonds' achievement was especially poignant given his father's deteriorating health. Once angered by reporters who mistakenly called him Bobby or who referred to him as the son of Bobby Bonds, Barry now displayed a caring affection for his father, rushing out of the locker room after games so that he could be with Bobby in the hospital as he recovered from surgery and pneumonia. Bobby's ill health also seemed to soften the way that sportswriters were treating Barry.

Of course, Bonds had not completely changed his image. He continued to maintain the singular ability to anger sports columnists even as he gained sympathy while his father battled cancer. His biggest moment of controversy in 2003 came in July during the All-Star break when reporters asked Bonds about his chances for breaking the all-time career home-run mark of 755 set by Hank Aaron. Bonds stated, "The only number I'll care about is Babe Ruth's. That's it—715. Because (that would mean) as a left-handed hitter, I wiped him out. That's it. And to the baseball world, Babe Ruth is Baseball, am I right? I got his slugging percentage and I'll take his home runs and that's it. Don't talk about him no more."[5]

Earlier in the summer, Bonds had visited the Negro Leagues Baseball Museum in Kansas City while the Giants played an interleague series against the

Royals. It was his first visit to the museum, and after a tour led by legendary Negro Leagues player Buck O'Neil, Bonds was reportedly greatly affected by the experience. Bonds mentioned his experience in Kansas City when he commented on Ruth. "You have a Negro Leagues museum over here in Kansas City, and you have a Hall of Fame over here [in Cooperstown, New York], and yet you tell me there's no segregation and discrimination in baseball? Why isn't there one institution? We, as future black Hall of Famers, or future minorities—even Hispanics—should recognize the Negro Leagues museum because we are an extension of that museum. We could put stuff in the regular Hall of Fame too, but we are an extension of that [Kansas City] museum." Bonds even put his own single-season home-run mark second to that of Josh Gibson's, who hit 84 in a single season while playing in the Negro Leagues but has never been recognized for the record.[6]

Not only did sports columnists attack Bonds for showing a lack of respect for Ruth, but some also said that his reverence toward the Negro Leagues Museum was less than genuine. A year earlier, Bonds did not show up at a dinner at the museum held in his honor, and sports columnists like Ross Newhan of the *Los Angeles Times* and Drew Olson of the *Milwaukee Journal Sentinel* talked about that in their criticisms of Bonds' remarks on Ruth. Newhan wrote that "as [Bonds] talked about wiping out Babe Ruth and about the importance of the Negro Leagues Baseball Museum in Kansas City, Missouri (an important museum, indeed, that Bonds had snubbed when it staged a dinner in his honor 17 months ago), I didn't view him as entertaining as much as insufferably arrogant and hypocritical."[7] Olson followed in a similar vein and added that he did not see why Bonds needed to put down Ruth to elevate the achievements of black ballplayers. "There is nothing wrong with bringing attention to Negro Leagues stars. Bonds chose to do it by belittling Babe Ruth, and that was inappropriate. Did Michael Jordan ever rip Bob Cousy? Would Michael Vick disrespect Fran Tarkenton?"[8]

The harshest criticism came from Michael Gibbons, the executive director of the Babe Ruth Birthplace Museum in Baltimore, who called Bonds' comments an "ill-conceived assault." In a written statement, Gibbon cited statistical evidence that he said proved Ruth's superiority over Bonds as a player. Gibbons attacked Bonds in a more personal manner, stating that he disregards "his role as baseball's natural good-will ambassador through an overt aloofness that turns off fans and players alike." Gibbons ended his statement by writing, "While you may in fact surpass Ruth's lifetime homers mark and rank as the all-time walks champion, to suggest that those feats are somehow capable of 'wiping out' Ruth illustrates a complete disregard for the history and tradition of our national game and its greatest player. Can Bonds 'wipe out' Ruth? Not today, not forever."[9]

As he had so often in the past, Bonds had made a great many sportswriters and fans indignant. He had not done so as much through any unethical actions or unseemly behavior, but through his words. Bonds' comments about Ruth not only showed a lack of respect that matched the image many already had of the Giants left fielder but also explicitly addressed the racial biases that are firmly embedded into baseball history like layers of sediment in stone formations. As much as Bonds had been attacked throughout his career in ways that reflect racial biases, he had never himself addressed race in such a direct way, nor in a forum like the All-Star Game, an event that is saturated with national media coverage and where any statement by a player like Bonds receives instant attention from national media outlets.

Comparisons between Ruth and Bonds are tinged with an undertone of racial history by definition. As Allan Barra had pointed out the previous October, one cannot even compare Ruth's numbers to Bonds' since Ruth played during the era of segregated baseball. Because of this, Ruth did not have to play against some of the greatest players in the game, either as a pitcher or as a hitter. Bonds (who, of course, would not have even been allowed to play in the major leagues during Ruth's time) plays not only against the best white and black ballplayers in the United States but also against many of the best players from Asia and Latin America as well.[10]

In a column that appeared two months after the All Star Game flap, ESPN columnist Ralph Wiley provided an insightful commentary upon it that addressed the issues of race involved. In an interesting cultural reference, Wiley drew upon the mythology of the American West to situate Bonds as a cultural icon. Wiley divided baseball players into two types: those belonging to the category of the "classic" ballplayer and those belonging to that of the "frontier."

> The Classic ballplayer is seen as having special, wondrous skills no one else could approach, and as a gregarious, lovable, hail-fellow-well-met, life-of-the-party, come-on-in-and-set-a-spell sort. Whether he is or not. The Frontier ballplayer is seen as distant, somehow unapproachable, grim, brusque, gruff, terse, downright ornery, lacking social graces, unwilling to bow to either prior convention or custom, and having attained from sheer implacable nature. Maybe between the lines sort of a bad guy, or leaning that way. Something about them causes a discomfort in the Eastern media elite.[11]

In Wiley's formulation, Barry Bonds is, of course, a frontier player, along with Ted Williams and Hank Aaron. Players like Babe Ruth, Joe DiMaggio, Willie Mays, and Ty Cobb Wiley list as classic. Wiley acknowledges the purely intuitive nature of such labels as "frontier" and "classic" and advises readers to remember that players are not, in reality, that different from one another. He notes that player reputations are largely the product of media spin and journalistic story lines. Race, he argues, is one of the most important issues that factors into how a player gets a reputation, and he argues that it was central to the anger that was directed against Bonds following the comments about Babe Ruth. He notes the irony that early in the Babe's career, Ty Cobb accused Ruth of being black and dismissed his greatness because he felt his skin color disqualified him from playing baseball. Ruth, Wiley writes, is "an icon so encompassing he could be seen as representative of a system of exclusion by one of his few historic peers (Bonds), and as an example of some liberal, let 'em-all-in disgrace by his main contemporary peer (Cobb)."

As Wiley notes, racists like Cobb wanted to dismiss Ruth's achievements on the field for reasons that had nothing to do with the game. In a biting comment that speaks to the criticism that many sports columnists have directed at Barry Bonds, Wiley writes, "And that is the very root of prejudice, bigotry, bias. The biased one will look for anything other than the craft at hand to examine." Wiley concludes, "No, Bonds isn't Willie Mays, or Henry Aaron, or Babe Ruth. As a hitter, he is, in fact, better. How we react to that fact says much more about us, and our biases, and where we are in life, than it does about Barry Bonds."[12]

The flap that erupted over Bonds' comments and the overt and covert racial messages involved in this story suggest that the position of African Americans in baseball continues to be a contentious issue. In fact, during the week of the All Star Game, *Sports Illustrated* published a story about the shrinking number of blacks playing baseball at any organized level and a "cultural disconnect" between the game and African American populations. Citing research conducted by Richard E. Lapchick from the Institute for Diversity and Ethics in Sport at the University of Central Florida, the article notes that the number of U.S.-born blacks in the major leagues had dropped from 27 percent in 1975 to 10 percent in 2002. There were more than twice as many African Americans named to the 1972 All-Star team (fifteen) than there were in 2002 (seven), and in 2002 there were only thirteen U.S.-born black pitchers in the major leagues, only five of whom were starters.[13] The article by Tom Verducci in *Sports Illustrated* notes that these numbers are the result of a lack of interest in baseball among African Americans and a lack of funding for grassroots programs that might generate an interest in baseball. Whatever the case might be, Bonds' own stardom and the kind of attention that he has received from sportswriters have not led to an outpouring of interest in baseball by African Americans.

Soon after the 2003 All-Star break, talk about Bonds' comments regarding Ruth died down, and Bonds continued to lead the Giants to an ever-expanding lead in the National League West. The team that had been expected to decline after the loss of Kent and Baker was walking away with the division title, led by Bonds, who had 40 home runs by early September. Two of his most memorable came during the third week of August in a key match-up against the Atlanta Braves, a team that many expected the Giants to meet in the National League Championship Series that fall. In the bottom of the 10th during the first game of the series, Bonds hit a game-winning home run into McCovey Cove. The next night, Bobby came to watch his son play, and the following night Barry hit another game-winning home run. Ned Colletti, the Giants assistant general manager said, "I've seen 500, 600, 650, 70, 71, and 73, and I'm telling you, that one was bigger and more special than all of them. It gave you chills. The guy doesn't pick up a bat for a week, he's spending time with his ill father, and the first day he comes back, he wins the game for us. He is special."[14]

Bobby was not there to see this last home run, and after the game, Barry rushed out of the clubhouse to be with his father. Bobby was able to watch his son the next night, but it was the last baseball game that he would ever attend. On August 23, Bobby Bonds died at the age of 57. Barry took a leave of absence, missing six games on bereavement leave to help take care of funeral arrangements and to be with his family. In a telling reversal of phrase, newspapers around the country reported that the *father* of Barry Bonds had died, reminding readers that he had once been a great major league player.[15] In accordance with the family's wishes, Bobby Bonds was laid to rest in private ceremonies—a wake in Burlingame, California, and a funeral service the next day across the bay in Hayward. A week later, over 500 admirers packed into a service in Bobby's hometown of Riverside, California, to honor their town's greatest athlete.[16]

In Bobby Bonds' obituary in *Sports Illustrated*, Ron Fimrite wrote that "he had heroically endured heart and brain surgeries and debilitating chemotherapy, often returning to Pac Bell Park for the last looks at the inheritor of his skills. Barry himself has frequently called attention to his father's courage. And as the son continues to topple records, researchers have discovered that the old man was himself a superior player and that his reputation as an underachiever was unfair."[17]

The death of his father did not hinder Bonds' performance, but it did seem to affect him. As Ken Rosenthal of the *Sporting News* wrote, "It's obvious Bonds cared deeply about his father."[18] Thomas Boswell added a note of understanding for Barry's often bitter moods and admiration for his abilities. "At the moment," Boswell wrote, "no one in any sport is as good as Bonds is at baseball. And few in any game have provided such heroics while in such emotional pain."[19]

In his first game back after his leave, Bonds hit his 40th home run of the season against Arizona Diamondbacks ace Randy Johnson. It was the margin of victory in the Giants 2–1 win, but the excitement and emotional stress also made Bonds take himself out of the game with an irregular heartbeat. The team reported that his heart was pounding at a rate of nearly 200 beats a minute, and Bonds was sent to the hospital for twenty-four hours.

Bonds recovered, and so did the Giants. Even with the loss of Bonds for roughly two weeks, the team finished with 100 wins for the first time since 1993, Bonds' first year with the Giants. Unlike 1993, however, the Giants won the Western Division and went to the playoffs. Bonds finished with outstanding numbers once more: a .341 batting average and .749 slugging percentage; 45 home runs; and a .529 on-base percentage. His 90 runs batted in were relatively low for his career, but he had a tremendous impact upon his team. By the end of the season, Bonds had not yet hit as many career home runs as his godfather, Willie Mays, but he was only 2 shy with a 658 total.

The Giants entered the first round of the playoffs as one of the favorites to win the National League pennant. They were scheduled to begin against a young, but scrappy, Florida Marlins team that had been counted out of any hope for making the postseason in April. Their manager, Jack McKeon, had vowed not to let Barry Bonds beat them in the playoffs, and he lived up to his promise. The Marlins walked Bonds 8 times (he ended up with only 9 official at-bats), and Bonds finished the series with a .222 average. The strategy worked. Despite having Bonds on base repeatedly, the team as a whole hit only .235, allowing their star to score only 3 times. After winning the opening game, the Giants lost the following three. The final two games were filled with errors and miscues, and the Marlins took full advantage of them to win the series. Florida then beat the Chicago Cubs in the League Championship Series and the New York Yankees in the World Series.

Nevertheless, Bonds was so instrumental to the Giants 100 regular season wins and their division championship that sportswriters voted him the National League Most Valuable Player for the third straight year and the sixth time in his career. He received 28 out of 32 first-place votes. This feat stands out among all Bonds' achievements. No other player in major league history has ever won more than three MVP awards total. Bonds told reporters after learning of the honor that this particular award stood out as the most meaningful one he has ever earned. "This is more special to me than any award I've ever received because it's dedicated to my father. . . . He has been my hitting coach my entire life, ever since I was a little kid. I miss him dearly. It's a really emotional time for me right now."[20]

As much as his sixth MVP award put a positive spin on a disappointing end to the season, Bonds also became implicated in an important controversy surrounding the use of performance-enhancing drugs. Shortly after the end of the World Series, investigators opened a probe against a Bay Area company called BALCO (Bay Area Laboratory Co-Operative) for producing a performance-enhancing steroid that was undetectable in ordinary tests administered to athletes to determine steroid use. Bonds had long endorsed BALCO for supplying him with nutritional supplements to increase his strength. His personal trainer, Greg Anderson, and BALCO founder, Victor Conte, were the only two people who were identified as targets in the probe. In early December, Bonds was called before a federal grand jury to investigate his connection to the company. Bonds was just one of many world-class athletes who were asked to testify, including sprinters Marion Jones and Tim Montgomery (the record holder in the 100-meter dash), four members of the Oakland Raiders, and Olympic gold medal swimmer Amy Van Dyken, yet Barry Bonds was the name that drew the most media attention. Not only was he the focus of publicity in the BALCO case, but he had become the key symbol for magazines, newspapers, television talking heads, and even politicians of the corruption in the world of sports brought about by the use of performance-enhancing drugs.[21]

NOTES

1. Ray Ratto, "All-Star Admits to Feeling It," *San Francisco Chronicle*, February 28, 2003, C1.

2. Jack Curry, "For Bonds, Life Is Wishing and Praying," *New York Times*, February 19, 2003, C1.

3. "Sports News," Associated Press, June 24, 2003.

4. Greg Beacham, "Bonds Might Remain 500-500 Club's Only Member," Associated Press, June 25, 2003.

5. Quoted in Drew Olson, "Bonds Drops the Ball," *Milwaukee Journal Sentinel*, July 20, 2003, 3C.

6. Quoted in Ross Newhan, "Bonds' Words Say Plenty," *Los Angeles Times*, July 20, 2003, 4.

7. Ibid.

8. Olson, "Bonds Drops the Ball," 3C.

9. Quoted in "Bonds Attacks, Bambinophiles Bash Back," *Newsday*, July 18, 2003, A73.

10. Allen Barra, "Barry and the Babe," Salon.com, October 25, 2002, http://archive.salon.com/news/sports/col/barra/2002/10/25/bonds/.

11. Ralph Wiley, "The Classic vs. The Frontier," ESPN.com, Page 2, September 10, 2003, http://espn.go.com/page2/s/wiley/030909.html.

12. Ibid.

13. Tom Verducci, "Blackout," *Sports Illustrated*, July 7, 2003, 56.

14. Tom Verducci, "More Valuable Than Ever," *Sports Illustrated*, September 1, 2003, 59.

15. Greg Beacham, "Bonds' Dad Dies," *(Memphis) Commercial Appeal*, August 24, 2003, C9; Richard Goldstein, "Bobby Bonds, 57, a Star and Father of Barry, Dies," *New York Times*, August 24, 2003, 35.

16. Jim Alexander, "Bonds Family: Private Times," *(Riverside) Press Enterprise*, August 28, 2003, F1; "Memorial Service Held for Bobby Bonds in His Hometown," Associated Press, September 5, 2003.

17. Ron Fimrite, "Remembering Bobby Bonds," *Sports Illustrated*, September 1, 2003, 59.

18. Ken Rosenthal, "Bonds Doesn't Need Sympathy Votes," *Sporting News*, September 1, 2003, 61.

19. Thomas Boswell, "A Son's Gift to His Father We All Can Share," *Washington Post*, September 3, 2003, D1.

20. Guy Curtright, "Emotions Strong for MVP Bonds," *Atlanta Journal-Constitution*, November 19, 2003, 3D.

21. Rob Gloster, "Bonds to Testify in Steroids Probe," *Harrisburg Patriot News*, December 4, 2003, C1.

"'ROID RAGE"

In mid-November 2003, Giants owner Peter Magowan asked team general manager Brian Sabean to propose a rule change at the annual general managers' meetings. The proposal called for a revision in the intentional walk rule so that a batter would be awarded one base for a first intentional walk during a game, two bases for a second, and three bases for a third. There was no information as to whether the Giants were proposing that a batter be awarded a home run for a fourth intentional walk, or whether it would be back to first again for a fifth. In any case, the other general managers quickly disposed of the proposed "Barry Bonds Rule," and the intentional walk procedure stayed intact.[1]

Nevertheless, given Bonds' dominant hitting over the previous four years, it did not seem likely that the rest of the league would vote for a rule that would increase his advantage on the playing field. Although a federal grand jury had implicated numerous athletes in the BALCO scandal, Bonds was at the center of it. Because Bonds' personal trainer Greg Anderson was one of the few people targeted in the probe, and because there had already been rumors that Bonds used steroids, media outlets suggested more openly than ever that Bonds' production was the result of performance-enhancing drugs.

Stories such as the Associated Press report on Bonds' testimony before the grand jury that appeared in the *Harrisburg (Pennsylvania) Patriot News* used photographs of Bonds at different points in his career to draw the link. In their article on the morning of his testimony, the *Patriot* editors showed a thin-looking Bonds from a 1996 file photo juxtaposed with a muscular, bald-headed Bonds from 2003. The caption below read, "These photos illustrate the physical changes in Giants slugger Barry Bonds over the last seven years."[2] Of course, in 1996, Bonds also hit 42 home runs, only 3 fewer than he did in 2003, and in 1993, he actually hit the third highest total of his career, knocking in 46 home runs. In addition, Bonds stated at the conclusion of the 2003 season that he would welcome steroid testing in Major League Baseball. In a conference call with reporters in November 2003, Bonds said, "I am glad that there is going to be testing. . . . I am glad that it will hopefully, hopefully diminish everyone's speculation and we'll be able to just move on."[3]

Unfortunately for Bonds, the BALCO case did not end so quickly. In early December, the grand jury called Bonds to testify. The secretive nature of the grand jury investigation only fueled speculation and interest among reporters and the general public. Bonds spent over five hours in the courtroom in San Francisco and said almost nothing to the crowd of reporters sent to witness the event when he arrived or when he left. When asked how the testimony had gone, Bonds simply answered, "fine." After he was done, his former teammate, catcher Benito Santiago, entered the chamber.[4]

As the grand jury deliberated over the winter holidays, fans and sportswriters speculated about the possible connections between Bonds' performance and illegal drugs. Ray Ratto, who covered Bonds' testimony, satirized the media hysteria that surrounded the connection between Bonds and BALCO. "And speaking of news," Ratto wrote as he described the reporters waiting outside the courtroom on the day Bonds testified, "at one point, an attorney handed out a release announcing the indictment of an Enron big shot on 11 counts of conspiracy and wire fraud (you know, real big-boy crime), causing a particularly eager media beagle to look at the release and say, 'What the hell do we need this for?'"[5]

Ratto may have been right to mock the fact that organizations entrusted with a responsibility to help create a "well informed public" were devoting so many resources to the Bonds–BALCO case, yet steroids and perhaps, by extension, Bonds had begun to enter into national political discourse in the wake of the BALCO scandal. In January 2004, some of the most noted words in President George W. Bush's State of the Union address were about steroids. "Unfortunately," said the president, "some in professional sports are not setting much of an example. The use of performance-enhancing drugs like steroids in baseball, football, and other sports is dangerous, and it sends the wrong message— that there are shortcuts to accomplishment and that performance is more important than character."[6]

Bush never mentioned Bonds in his reference to steroids in the State of the Union address. However, Bonds was a clear, if not explicit, symbol invoked in the president's statement about "shortcuts to accomplishment." It is noteworthy, for example, that the president mentioned baseball first in his address. This is not surprising since George W. Bush was once a controlling shareholder of the Texas Rangers baseball team, and given baseball's nationwide popularity yet he also never mentioned track and field, lumping it into a broad category of "other sports," even though a number of athletes connected with BALCO are Olympic sprinters. In fact, for many sports authorities around the globe, the involvement of track athletes with steroids is a far more serious issue than the particular case of Barry Bonds. International agencies have long felt that the U.S. Olympic Committee has not done enough to police the use of steroids among American Olympic athletes.[7]

In raising the steroids issue, the president likely sought to portray himself as someone interested in protecting the moral character of traditional institutions in the United States. According to reports, this was the reason the president himself brought up the issue of steroids when his staff was planning his speech. According to political columnist Jeff Greenfield, "the topic first came up when the staff was discussing the policy outline for the speech." As reported by Greenfield, an unnamed presidential staffer recalled the following: "We were talking about a portion of the speech—the moral integrity of social institutions. We had stuff on high school drug-testing. The President said, 'What about the moral messages sent by adults?' . . . He has a unique perspective on this. His father played baseball. He was a team owner. He doesn't like fake home runs."[8]

The implications of this report from an anonymous source are important. If steroids are seen as a symbol of moral decline in America, and if Barry Bonds is seen as a symbol of steroid use in baseball, then Bonds, by extension, had become a political target within the current culture wars. Saying that the president does not like "fake home runs" points an accusatory finger at Bonds without ever having to say his name and makes him responsible for a host of social ills for his alleged and as yet unproven indiscretion with steroids. Even within the game of baseball, the president's rhetorical maneuver and his aide's recollection of the speechwriting session suggest that only players want to be on steroids, thereby ignoring the many ways that owners themselves have been complicit with the steroid problem in baseball.

The BALCO case further integrated itself into the cultural politics of the day on February 12, 2004, when the grand jury handed down a forty-two-count indictment of BALCO executives. Rather than issue a press release, the federal Justice Department called a press conference in Washington, D.C., where U.S. attorney general John Ashcroft announced the charges. Ashcroft told reporters that four individuals affiliated with BALCO were being charged with illegal distribution of steroids and other performance-enhancing drugs to athletes, possession of human growth hormone, and money laundering. Since anabolic steroids are a controlled substance, it is illegal to distribute them without a doctor's prescription. Bonds was not among the indicted, but those who were had worked closely with him and were people whom he credited with much of his success. Greg Anderson and BALCO founder Victor Conte Jr. were both indicted along with BALCO vice president James J. Valente and track coach Remi Korchemny. In a prepared statement that he read out loud, Ashcroft said, "Illegal steroid use calls into question not only the integrity of the athletes who use them, but also the integrity of the sports that those athletes play. Steroids are bad for sports, they're bad for players, they're bad for young people who hold athletes up as role models."[9]

News reports had alleged that the four had not only produced and distributed steroids but also developed a new form of steroid called THG that, until the fall of 2003, was not detectable through standard forms of drug testing. The government alleged that BALCO had sold THG and other such substances to dozens of professional athletes. Already, nine athletes had tested positive for THG.[10]

All this took place just as spring training opened, and it seemed to cast a pall over the Giants arrival in Scottsdale, Arizona, where even the weather on February 23 was cold, wet, and gloomy, yet if Bonds felt depressed by the BALCO story, he showed no signs of it. Reporters saw a happy, joking Barry Bonds, a mood that he often displayed during the first days of training camp. Unlike Jason Giambi of the New York Yankees, who raised eyebrows and suspicions about steroid use when he showed up for camp considerably thinner than the year before, reporters noted that Bonds was as muscular as ever. When asked if he was disturbed that some people might discount his records because of the belief that he was taking steroids, he replied, "There's nothing I can do about it right now. Better go on to other questions." When a writer asked if he favored mandatory drug testing, Bonds responded just as he had on earlier occasions. "They can test me every day if they want to."[11]

Bonds spent most of his time with reporters discussing how he was coping without his father. For the first time in his career, Bonds came to training camp without Bobby, who had been his mentor and hitting coach. This year, Willie Mays came as his guardian and source of wisdom. Bonds revealed to reporters that he had spent much of the off-season talking to Mays and to Hank Aaron about their home-run records and about the possibility that he might surpass them. "Just being with my godfather trying to go through the healing process without my father, just through our conversations and his support of me in the wintertime has changed my outlook on a lot of things. . . . I broke down a couple of times in the batting cage because of the fact he wasn't with me. . . . He's been my coach my whole life. The best thing about it is, Willie has taken that role for me now and he's been working out with me three days a week in the wintertime and easing the pain for me to go through the process without my father."[12]

Bonds concluded with one of the most positive statements about playing baseball that he has ever made to reporters. "This is what I love to do. I'm proud of being a Giant, proud of wearing this uniform, proud of playing baseball. Regardless of what my problems are or what situations are at hand, they're still going to be there anyway. Baseball has been more of a stress relief than anything else. Baseball has been time away from everything. It's something I enjoy. I enjoy it for the fans and enjoy it for myself. I enjoy being on the stage."[13]

Mays, displaying more the pride of a godfather than the jealousy of a competitor, showed reporters a diamond-studded Olympic torch that he had carried to the 1996 Olympics and that he was planning to give Bonds at the moment that his godson surpassed his own career home-run mark of 660. The torch is inscribed with the words "Barry Bonds, no. 25, 660 to 661." "If I have to, I will try to do my best to be there because I've got other things to do, but he's my first priority right now because he needs the help."[14]

Unfortunately, it did not take long for the positive tone of training camp to shatter. First, Colorado Rockies pitcher Turk Wendell told reporters during training camp that he believed Bonds was guilty of taking illegal steroids. Wendell said, "If my personal trainer, me, Turk Wendell, got indicted for that, there's no one in the world who wouldn't think that I wasn't taking steroids. . . . I mean, what, because he's Barry Bonds, no one's going to say that? I mean obviously he did it. . . . (His trainer) admitted to giving steroids to baseball players. He just doesn't want to say his name. You don't have to. It's clear just seeing his body."[15]

Aside from being the first player to openly accuse Bonds of using steroids, Wendell is perhaps the first person to have ever accused Bonds of receiving unfairly favorable treatment in the press. Nevertheless, teammate Denny Neagle reiterated Wendell's accusations. "It is a pretty good coincidence that some of the names that are linked to (steroids) are the guys that are the big, massive, over-muscular-looking guys. And guys that did go through some serious body changes. I don't know or remember what (New York Yankees first baseman) Jason Giambi looked like back in his early days, but I know he wasn't as big as he is now. The jury is always going to be out on Barry."[16]

Bonds responded angrily. He told reporters, "You know what? If you've got something to say, say it to my face. Don't be a little pussy and talk to the media. If you've got something to say to me, come to my face and say it and we'll handle it amongst ourselves, but don't talk to the media. I'm tired of that. I'm tired of guys chirping through the media." Bonds continued, "I'm not worried about

(Wendell). I don't worry about any of them. I have a lot of respect for Turk Wendell. I have a lot of respect for every baseball player in this game. Just to disrespect other people like that, or talk to the media, I think that's chickens—. If you've got something to say, you come to my face and say it, and we'll deal with each other, but don't be a pussy and go talk to the media like you're some tough guy."[17]

Over the course of the BALCO controversy, however, Bonds' own words to the media were more incriminating than Wendell's accusations. Sportswriters discovered an interview and feature article in Muscle & Fitness Online, in which Bonds had praised BALCO, and credited the troubled company with his success at the plate at a relatively late time in life.

> Working with personal trainer Greg Anderson, the superstar slugger has refined his weight training and nutrition regimens, and it shows. "Definitely, my improvements as a player are down to training and nutrition. . . . Without a doubt. It has made me a better athlete than I was before."[18]

The article continues in this manner, quoting Bonds as crediting indicted BALCO executives with supplying crucial dietary supplement regimens.

> Bonds' rejuvenation owes itself to more than sets and reps. He's now calibrating his athletic performance at the cellular level. Since winter of 2000, Bonds has worked closely with San Francisco-based nutritional consultant Victor Conte of BALCO Laboratories. Conte precisely measures the nutrient levels in the outfielder's blood, then prescribes specific supplemental regimens to correct imbalances. Like the managers of every National League team, Bonds has noticed the difference. "I'm just shocked by what they've been able to do for me," he says. "Before I didn't understand how important these nutrient levels were, because I was just listening to old standard nutritionists who tell you to just eat 4,000 calories a day. Everyone's body changes over time, and every individual is different. To have your blood drawn and analyzed can tell you what your body produces more of, what it lacks. You're able to create a program that fits for you as an individual. . . . People don't understand how important this is," he explains. "I visit BALCO every three to six months. They check my blood to make sure my levels are where they should be. Maybe I need to eat more broccoli than I normally do. Maybe my zinc and magnesium intakes need to increase, and I need more ZMA. Nobody every showed it to me in a scientific way before, how important it is to balance your body. I have that knowledge now."[19]

The article contains a link to a Web page that provides the "home run work-out routine for Giants slugger, Barry Bonds." It lists the multitude of vitamins, minerals, and dietary supplements that he takes on a daily basis. Anabolic steroids and THG are, of course, not listed, yet the article only further advanced suspicions that many already had about Bonds' relationship to performance-enhancing drugs. If the court of public opinion had ever held Bonds as innocent until proven guilty, those days were over. Sportswriters, editors, and many fans now presumed Bonds to be guilty and saw his achievements as suspect.

On March 15, 2004, *Sports Illustrated* published a special issue on steroids in baseball. The issue's cover featured a full frontal shot of Bonds' face, an image that occupied most of the frame with the magazine logo superimposed over the top of his bald head. Bonds looks up and to his right, his brow furrowed, with a worried expression upon his somewhat bloated-looking face. The headline of the magazine asks, "Is baseball in the asterisk era?" It is a reference to Roger Maris' single-season home-run record of 61 that he set for the New York Yankees in 1961, surpassing the 60 home runs that Babe Ruth hit in 1927. During Maris' time, baseball commissioner Ford Frick had the official record books put an asterisk by Maris' number because he had accomplished his feat during a 162-game season while Ruth had played only a 154-game schedule. On the cover, there is a large watermark of an asterisk on Bonds' forehead above his left eye while a footnote in the bottom right-hand corner of the magazine cover reads, "All power records subject to suspicion. Is it fair?"[20]

The feature article inside begins with a two-page photo spread of Bonds finishing a graceful swing during a game at Pac Bell Park. The camera angle is from behind and below Bonds as he twists his body, his right leg extended straight, his left bent so that his weight is on his toe. He is looking off in the distance as if to follow the trajectory of a baseball that he has just hit. Although the caption does not tell us what is happening in the picture, it is easy to imagine that Bonds has just hit a home run, perhaps even the record-breaking home run that he hit in 2001 to set the single-season record at 73. The photo is black and white, which not only gives it a dark and troubling look but reminds those who view it of other historic photographs of baseball players. The black-and-white image is a visual code. Because it looks "historic," it makes readers think about how people in the future will look upon the accomplishments of contemporary baseball players. This image complements the question raised by the headline, "Is baseball in the asterisk era? New questions about steroids have cast doubt on the legitimacy of the game's power-hitting records."[21]

In the feature article, Tom Verducci writes, "When Bonds hits number 661 to pass Mays, his godfather, the historic event will engender as much debate as celebration. Bonds will reach the milestone with his personal trainer, Greg Anderson, under indictment for the illegal distribution of steroids and human growth hormone (HGH). . . . The past decade has been the greatest extended run of slugging the game has witnessed. At the same time it has been the first decade of documented steroid use in baseball. . . . The temptation to connect those dots fuels the growing debate." The article continues by quoting baseball commissioner Bud Selig as saying that he would consider putting an asterisk by the records of any player who was found to have used steroids. Verducci ends by describing the scene in spring training when Bonds came to bat in his first game. "As Bonds stepped to the plate in his first exhibition at bat last week, at the Chicago Cubs spring training home in Mesa, Ariz., the crowd's reaction to him might well have been a referendum on these boom times in baseball. Many of the fans cheered. More of them booed. One man held a sign that said, EVERYBODY KNOWS THAT STEROIDS PRODUCE NUMBERS."[22]

The *Sports Illustrated* issue calls into question not only Bonds' numbers but the entire surge of home-run production within the game of baseball during the 1990s. It suggests that there is a connection between this increased production and the first documented use of steroids within Major League Baseball. This documentation occurred during the 2003 season when, following an agreement with the Major League Player's Association, Major League Baseball tested each of more than 1,400 players. According to the agreement, the results of the testing were to remain confidential. However, if more than 5 percent of players would test positive, then punishments would be imposed during the 2004 season.[23] After the testing was completed, between 5 and 7 percent of players had positive results.[24]

As much as media outlets like *Sports Illustrated* addressed the steroid problem in baseball as a general one, they also made Bonds the central image of this problem. Gary Sheffield and Jason Giambi were also BALCO clients, but the magazine cover alone made obvious what most baseball fans already were thinking: Barry Bonds had become the face of steroids. Bonds, however, continued to deny that he had ever used steroids, and as rumors continued to leak about Bonds and BALCO, lawyers for the indicted defendants tried to take some pressure off Bonds. J. Tony Serra, attorney for Greg Anderson, called a news conference to announce that Bonds had refused steroids when they had been offered to him. Serra told reporters that a calendar had been found in Victor Conte's office with Barry Bonds' name on it, listing Bonds as a player who was to begin using a performance-enhancing drug. Bonds, according to Serra, refused to take it. "Barry Bonds never took anything illegal, and my client never provided him anything that the government claims is illegal," Serra told reporters. "My client is loyal to him, and Barry Bonds took no illegal substances." Voctor Conte's lawyer, Robert Holley, supported Serra's statement. "My client knows of no illegal activity that has ever been done by Barry Bonds. (Conte) would like us to go on record because of the rumors and innuendos."[25]

Less than a week later, however, reports of the BALCO investigation directly fingered Bonds for the first time. Reporters Lance Williams and Mark Fainaru-Wada of the *San Francisco Chronicle* broke a front-page story alleging that Bonds, Jason Giambi, Gary Sheffield, former Giants Marvin Benard and Benito Santiago, major league second baseman Randy Velarde, and football linebacker Bill Romanowski had all received illegal, performance-enhancing drugs from BALCO. Williams and Fainaru-Wada received their information from court documents leaked to them from the grand jury investigation. The reporters confirmed the information about Bonds with an anonymous source who knew Greg Anderson and who told the reporters that Bonds had been receiving illegal, performance-enhancing drugs since 2001, the season that he had hit 73 home runs. The article did not confirm whether Bonds had ever actually used these drugs. Bonds' attorney, Michael Rains, questioned the credibility of the *Chronicle*'s source and once more denied that Bonds had used steroids. "We continue to adamantly deny that Barry was provided, furnished or supplied any of those substances at any time by Greg Anderson," Rains told reporters.[26]

The chief investigator for the inquiry was Jeff Novitzky, an agent for the Internal Revenue Service. He alleged that Anderson and Conte had confessed to him the names of players to whom they had provided steroids. Novitzky wrote in an affidavit, "Anderson admitted that he had given steroids to several professional baseball players whose names I was familiar with from my review of other documents in this case." No players' names were released to reporters, however, and references to players were deleted from public court files as part of an immunity pledge made by players who agreed to testify before the grand jury.[27] With the *Chronicle* report, however, the public was finally able to see names connected with the investigation, names that many had suspected were linked to steroids all along.

The day after the *Chronicle* story appeared, Bonds avoided reporters. The only statement that he did make reflected his own sense of frustration over the media circus surrounding the steroids issue. "The most wanted man in America," Bonds told reporters as he walked by them on his way to the locker room. He then raised his hand in a fist and said, "Black power." Meanwhile, U.S. representative John Sweeney, a Republican representing the district that includes Cooperstown, New York, introduced legislation to add a number of currently legal substances, such as androstenedione (which Mark McGwire publicly acknowledged using) to the list of Schedule II Controlled Substances. Sweeney also added that he thought an asterisk should be placed next to the names of players "involved in illegal substances."[28]

By the end of March, even conservative political television host Bill O'Reilly from the Fox News Channel had *jumped on the bandwagon* declaring Bonds and steroids a threat to the nation's moral fabric. On March 24, O'Reilly had on John Salley and Tom Arnold, hosts of Fox Sports Network's *The Best Damn Sports Show Period*. Throughout the program, O'Reilly badgered his guests to concede that athletes on steroids were setting a poor example for the nation's youth, while Salley and Arnold, attempting to articulate a slightly more nuanced understanding of the problem, kept backing themselves into a corner by defending the use of steroids by athletes. Finally, O'Reilly addressed the example of Barry Bonds directly.

O'Reilly: But here's the bigger picture. When the fans go to the game this year, you know, and Barry Bonds walks out of the dugout, you know, people are going to say he cheated. He cheated.

Arnold: Who's going to say that? I'm not going to—we don't know that for sure.

O'Reilly: No, but . . .

Arnold: The other . . .

O'Reilly: . . . fans are going to say he cheated period. They are.

Arnold: So what? So what?

Salley: Is that going to make him hit the—the steroids give you muscles. Is that going to make you see the ball better? No.

Arnold: His wrists are so—his wrists—it's all wrist speed with Barry Bonds, and steroids hurt your wrist speed. Look at . . .

O'Reilly: Oh, don't give me any of that business. You bulk up on that stuff . . .

Arnold: That's true.

Salley: It doesn't make your eyes better, Bill.[29]

O'Reilly is well known for interrupting and badgering his guests to get his point across. In this particular case, his focus is less the health and well-being of young athletes who might take a dangerous synthetic hormone, and more the moral character of Bonds, whom he called a "cheater" three times. Whether Bonds may have used steroids or not is almost not relevant to this kind of television talk show debate. What is important is how a personality like O'Reilly targeted Bonds, making him a stand-in for a wide range of social ills linked to a perceived decline in national character.

Although media attention in the BALCO case focused heavily upon Barry Bonds, he was still not the official target of the federal investigation and trial. The only people to have been charged were the BALCO executives named in the indictment, yet as reporters began to cover the story more extensively, stories began to emerge that suggested Bonds was the target of the federal probe from the beginning. In late March, *Playboy* magazine posted an article on its Web site that was to appear in the April 9 edition. It alleged that Jeff Novitsky, the Internal Revenue Service (IRS) agent in charge of the BALCO investigation, had initiated the probe after he himself had, begun working out at Greg Anderson's gym. The article quotes a Bureau of Narcotics Enforcement officer named Iran White, who said that Novitsky noticed Bonds' extremely muscular body and decided to find out if he was on steroids. According to White, Novitsky was not at all an impartial detective but instead had a personal vendetta against Bonds. White says that Novitsky told him that he wanted to show that Bonds had been taking steroids. "He's such (a jerk) to the press. I'd sure like to prove it," Novitsky allegedly told White.[30]

White had been part of the BALCO investigation and had gone undercover as a bodybuilder in an attempt to get close to Anderson. Despite wearing a hidden recording device, he was never able to gather any statement from Anderson that would have provided incriminating evidence that he was distributing steroids. After suffering a stroke, White left the case.[31] Most of the evidence gathered came from the work of Novitzky, who examined the garbage outside the BALCO offices once a week over the course of several months. In a fifty-two-page affidavit, Novitzky said that in the trash he had found empty boxes of the anabolic steroids testosterone, Oxandrin; vials of serostin, a human growth hormone; and incriminating letters.[32] Anna Ling, an attorney on Anderson's defense team, cast doubt on the investigation, noting how much of the government's case had been built upon the investigative work of one detective whose credibility she questioned. Ling told reporters that the allegations made in the *Playboy* article would figure in her client's defense. " 'It looks like Novitsky started this investigation," she told reporters. She added that the investigation of BALCO "was inspired or began with the purpose of bringing down Barry Bonds for whatever reason. That is a very personal motive."[33]

Bonds continued to stay quiet around reporters when the topic turned to steroids or BALCO. On April 6, opening night of the 2004 season, however, he spoke loudly with his bat. In the eighth inning against Roy Oswalt and the Houston Astros, Bonds hit his first pitch over the right-field fence. He also hit two doubles and drove in three runs. The home run put his career total at 659, just one behind his godfather, Willie Mays, who was in attendance that night at Houston's Minutemaid Field. It was the sixth time in Bonds' major league career that he had hit a home run on opening day.[34]

That same day, however, steroid news continued to shadow Bonds' on-field achievements. Federal prosecutors had issued a subpoena seeking to gain access to urine samples from the testing that took place in 2003 to see if any came back positive in tests for THG, the steroid that had previously been undetectable in conventional lab tests. Of the 1,400 players who were tested the previous year, all but 500 samples were destroyed. Major League Baseball refused to retest the samples.[35]

On April 8, federal authorities raided the offices of Quest Diagnostics in Las Vegas, the lab that conducted the steroid tests for Major League Baseball. They seized documentation and specimens consistent with their subpoena just after the Major League Players Association had filed a motion in San Francisco seeking to invalidate the subpoena. The players' association's objections were based upon their collective bargaining agreement with Major League Baseball, which stated that the tests were meant to remain anonymous. It was not known if Bonds' sample was among the roughly 500 seized by agents.[36]

On the field, Bonds' bat quieted down. During the Giants opening road trip, Mays had followed his godson to every game, ready to present the silver torch at the moment that Bonds hit home-run number 660. Amid the media hype, Bonds strained to hit one out of the ballpark that would make him the third most prolific career home-run hitter in baseball history. Despite coming close, Bonds ended opening road trips against Houston and San Diego still at 659, getting 3 hits in 16 at-bats and walking 6 times in 5 games. Fans in San Diego chanted "Balco! Balco!" each time Bonds stepped to the plate, while fans in the outfield stands held up handmade signs that spelled out the word B-A-L-C-O as Bonds took his position in left field.[37]

Bonds stepped onto the home field in San Francisco on Monday, April 12, with a more supportive crowd cheering for him. Before the game, hockey Hall of Famer Wayne Gretsky and basketball Hall of Fame center Bill Russell presented Bonds with his sixth Most Valuable Player award in a ceremony behind home plate. In the fifth inning, on a 3–1 pitch from Matt Kinney of the Milwaukee Brewers, Bonds hit a three-run home run over the right field wall, into McCovey Cove. The accomplishment may someday have an asterisk beside it, but Barry Bonds had finally reached one of his most precious achievements. He had tied his hero and godfather's career home-run record.[38]

The game was suspended for a few moments so that Mays could greet Bonds after he crossed home plate and present him with the silver torch. The two embraced and posed for pictures. Bonds later took a curtain call, stepping out of the dugout and waving to the fans who chanted back "Barry! Barry!" Bonds said, "It's a great honor to do this today, in front of our hometown fans, to have Willie here. . . . I felt I was pushing myself a little bit with Willie with me, traveling. Willie kept telling me, 'I'm okay, don't worry about me.' Willie is my mentor. As an athlete, to have someone like Willie Mays with you is amazing."[39]

After the game, Bonds told reporters, "Right now, this is a great accomplishment for myself. . . . I'm not going to try to figure out what's going to happen next. . . . It was like a weight was just lifted off my shoulders. It's a relief now to be able to stand next to my godfather and finally feel like I've accomplished something in the game of baseball. It was a big way of getting his approval that I've finally done something."

Mays said of his godson, "I wanted him to get it over with—that was no. 1. . . . When Barry swings hard, nothing happens. If you looked at his swing today, it was an easy, compact swing and the ball went a long ways. In Houston and San Diego, he was trying to lift the ball to give it a little help." It was the 28th time that Bonds had hit a home run into McCovey Cove, and, unlike his 73rd home run, there was no controversy over what would happen to the ball. Larry Ellison, the fan who fished the ball out of the bay, returned it to Bonds, who kept it as the most treasured souvenir of his career.[40]

Nevertheless, almost every newspaper article describing Bonds' home run also mentioned the ongoing steroid probe. Sports commentators called it the "steroid cloud" that hung over Bonds' career. Even if it is true that Bonds takes steroids, the attention that he receives far outshines that of any other athlete currently under investigation in the same probe. What the allegations of steroid use do imply is that Bonds has reached his achievements on the field unfairly, and, given his reputation as an unlikable player, this is something that many sportswriters and fans clearly seem to want to believe. Beyond his own actual guilt or innocence in this probe, the public interest in Bonds' involvement with steroids goes beyond the fact that he is an accomplished baseball player. It is also connected to the images and stories associated with Bonds, which themselves are the product of a long history of ideas associated with sports and race in the United States.

NOTES

1. Carl Steward, " 'Barry Bonds rule' Was a Giant Farce," *Alameda Times-Star*, November 22, 2003.

2. Rob Gloster, "Bonds to Testify in Steroids Probe," *Harrisburg Patriot News*, December 4, 2003, C1.

3. Mike Klis, "Bonds Wins Sixth MVP," *Denver Post*, November 19, 2003, D01.

4. Lance Williams and Mark Fainaru-Wada, "Slugger Testifies in Steroids Probe," *San Francisco Chronicle*, December 5, 2003, A1.

5. Ray Ratto, "Waiting for Barry like Day at Park," *San Francisco Chronicle*, December 5, 2003, C1.

6. John Shea, "Bush Calls for Pro Sports to End Use of Steroids," *San Francisco Chronicle*, January 29, 2004, A15.

7. Jack Curry, "Drug Testing: Four Indicted in a Steroid Scheme That Involved Top Pro Athletes," *New York Times*, February 13, 2004.

8. Jeff Greenfield, "Can the Government Clean Up the Game?" *Sports Illustrated*, March 15, 2004, 44.

9. Curry, "Drug Testing: Four Indicted in a Steroid Scheme That Involved Top Pro Athletes."

10. Ibid.

11. T. J. Quinn, "Bonds: Test Me Every Day Bonds Denies Drug Use," *New York Daily News*, February 24, 2004, 71.

12. Henry Shulman, " 'The New Say Hey Kid': With Mays in Support, Bonds Set to Embark on His Toughest Season," *San Francisco Chronicle*, February 24, 2001, C1.

13. Ibid.

14. Ibid.

15. Henry Schulman, "Rockies Pitcher Accuses Bonds," *San Francisco Chronicle*, February 26, 2004, A1.

16. Ibid.

17. Ibid.

18. "What Fuels Baseball Superhitter Barry Bonds?" Muscle & Fitness Online, http://www.muscle-fitness.com/feature/3?page=2.

19. "A Home Run Workout Routine from Giants Slugger, Barry Bonds," http://www.muscle-fitness.com/training/4?page=2.

20. Cover, *Sports Illustrated*, March 15, 2004.

21. Tom Verducci, "Is Baseball in the Asterisk Era?" *Sports Illustrated*, March 15, 2004, 36–37.

22. Ibid.

23. "Baseball Notes," *Harrisburg Patriot News*, April 6, 2004, C4.

24. Neal Conan (Host), "Steroids in Athletics," *Talk of the Nation*, National Public Radio, February 18, 2004.

25. Lance Williams and Mark Fainaru-Wada, "Two Lawyers Say Bonds Never Took Illegal Drugs," *San Francisco Chronicle*, February 28, 2004, A5.

26. Lance Williams and Mark Fainaru-Wada, "Bonds Got Steroids, Feds Were Told," *San Francisco Chronicle*, March 2, 2004, A1.

27. Ibid.

28. Lance Williams and Mark Fainaru-Wada, "Bonds Embraces Outlaw Status," *San Francisco Chronicle*, March 3, 2004, A5.

29. "Interview with 'Best Damn Sports Show Period' Co-Hosts John Salley, Tom Arnold," *The O'Reilly Factor*, Fox News, March 24, 2004.

30. Quoted in Mike Klis, "Playboy Article Could Shift Focus," Denver Post.Com, March 28, 2004, http://www.denverpost.com/Stories/0,1412,36-108-2046742,00.html.

31. Pete Carey and Elliott Almond, "Attorney Says *Playboy* Report Undermines Investigation," San Jose Mercury News.com, March 25, 2004, http://www.mercurynews.com/mld/mercurynews/sports/8268684.htm?1c.

32. Curry, "Drug Testing: Four Indicted in a Steroid Scheme That Involved Top Pro Athletes."

33. Mike Klis, "Attorney Says *Playboy* Report Undermines Investigation," Denver Post.com.

34. "Bonds Closing on Mays," *Harrisburg Patriot News*, April 6, 2004, C4.

35. "Baseball Notes," *Harrisburg Patriot News*, April 6, 2004, C4.

36. "Feds Seize Baseball Drug Test Results, Samples," AOL Sports News, April 9, 2004, http://aolsvc.news.aol.com/sportss/article.adp?id=20040409195909990002.

37. "An Offering Bonds Can't Refuse," *Los Angeles Times*, April 13, 2004, D1.

38. Ibid.

39. Ibid.

40. Ibid.

Barry Bonds and his godfather, Willie Mays, speak at a press conference in San Francisco after Bonds hit his 660th home run against the Milwaukee Brewers on April 12, 2004. The home run tied Bonds with Mays on Major League Baseball's career home-run list. © *Reuters/CORBIS*.

EPILOGUE

On April 13, 2004, the night after Barry Bonds hit home-run number 660 to tie Willie Mays, he put himself in sole possession of third place on the all-time home-run list. With the bases empty and the count at one ball and two strikes in the seventh inning, Bonds hit a slider from Milwaukee Brewers relief pitcher Ben Ford over the right field wall and into McCovey Cove. The ball traveled 468 feet. Once again, Larry Ellison fished it out of the murky, cold waters of San Francisco Bay. This time he kept it. It did not matter much to Bonds. "Six-sixty was the one," Bonds said after the game. "That's the one that will be on my desk forever. I don't feel I'm ahead of Willie because Willie is my mentor. He always will be. . . . I still feel he's the greatest player of all time. That hasn't changed." Then Bonds smiled for the press and added, "They were saying my dad was the next Willie Mays. They just got the name wrong, from Bobby to Barry."[1]

Toward the end of the 2003 season, John Rawlings and Ron Smith of the *Sporting News* conducted a point–counterpoint debate over who will go down in baseball history as the better player, Willie Mays or Barry Bonds. Smith wrote in favor of Mays and cited his base-stealing prowess—which earned Mays four stolen base championships—and his outstanding defense in center field. Rawlings, arguing for Bonds, wrote, "Bonds has constructed a career in which numbers tell only part of the story. . . . Bonds has four seasons already in which his slugging percentage is better than the best Mays ever posted, and this season will be the fifth. . . . Mays drew 1,464 walks in his career; Bonds already has a staggering 2,061 and more every day. By the numbers, Bonds has fewer chances to hit, and he makes more of them. How else can you judge two hitters side-by-side?" Both writers ended their arguments with judgmental statements about Bonds not as a baseball player but as a human being. Smith wrote, "Most Bonds–Mays comparisons focus on home runs, Gold Gloves, MVPs and five-tool abilities. But Mays used a sixth tool Bonds does not possess. He played with a smile." Rawlings writes, "I don't like Barry Bonds, but whether I like him is not the point. Understanding he will end his career as the second-best player in the history of the game is."[2]

After Bonds hit home-run number 660, Allen Wilson of the *Buffalo News* wrote a column that once more focused upon Bonds' personality. Noting that Bonds lives under a "cloud of suspicion" due to his alleged use of steroids, Wilson suggested that the slugger's personality makes it harder for fans to forgive him. "He comes off as unapproachable with his don't-bother-me attitude. His child-like petulance and arrogance have been turnoffs for the media and baseball fans." Like Rawlings and Smith, Wilson contrasted Bonds' personality to that of Mays. "Unlike Mays, Bonds may never be able to garner all the accolades and love worthy of a sports icon."[3]

Since the middle of the nineteenth century and the emergence of such cultural ideals as "muscular Christianity," people in the United States have connected sports to moral development and character building. In actual fact, sports embody deep social contradictions, as sociologist D. Stanley Eitzen has illustrated. For example, when winning is framed within popular cultural ideals associated with something like Horatio Alger stories, it is easy to see victory as a sign not only of ability or training but also of high moral character, yet because winning is so highly valued in the sports culture that has developed in the United States, cheating to win is not only common but often encouraged.

Thus, fans want those who win to be those who they think, for whatever reason, *deserve* to win, not only for their on-field performance but because of the character that fans think an athlete might embody. This trend has become even more pronounced over the past sixty years, a time in American history that has been defined by enormous social transformation. As historian Henry Yu has pointed out, one of the key components of this historical change has been the emergence of a consumer culture in which sports are a central component. While sports in the United States emerged at a time in the nineteenth century when there was a clear differentiation between work and play, "the twentieth century saw a remarkable transition in the United States and other advanced capitalist nations . . . where the difference between work and play seemed much less clear." Yu noted that this tremendous social change is largely the product of mass consumption fueled by entertainment and mass media. The increasingly intense glare of the media spotlight has created the phenomenon of media celebrity, with most images of celebrity being those of sports stars. According to Yu, "by the end of the twentieth century . . . in the popular imagination, moral character in a heroic sense was almost monopolized by sports figures," much in the way that war leaders in the past have been able to translate their battlefield heroics into political careers based upon their perceived moral character. Citing the criminal trials of high-profile athletes, Yu argues that these reveal not a decline in the moral character of athletes (after all, sports figures have been implicated in morally questionable behavior since the beginning of professional sports) but a desire among Americans for their star athletes "to be heroes in ways that were not required fifty years before."[4]

Often, successful professional athletes work hard to develop an image off the field that matches the ideal that fans want to see in their winners. Michael Jordan and Tiger Woods are prime examples of sports personalities who have done this very successfully. Each appears before the public as gracious and polite, people who seem to be not only winners within the arena of sports but deserving of admiration as human beings as well. Of course, such images might only be the product of public relations consultation, but for Jordan and Woods, they have created a fit between their athletic prowess and what fans want to believe are their personal characters.

Sometimes there is a contradiction between public images created for athletes and the private lives that they actually live. This happened in the summer of 2003 when it was revealed that former Minnesota Twins Hall of Fame outfielder Kirby Puckett had an abusive relationship with his wife. Puckett had cultivated a "positive" image that his fans believed—he was a good "community man" who signed autographs, played hard, showed up at charity events, and never complained. Fans embraced him not only because he won but because he also created a public image of high moral character that matched his athletic abilities. When *Sports Illustrated* published details of accusations that Puckett had hit his wife, it was particularly disturbing for his fans. They had cheered him not only because he was good but because he seemed to represent positive values and good moral character.

Barry Bonds has never worked very hard at developing a public image. Toward the end of the 1990s, many noticed that he had begun to "mellow" a bit. He talked to more reporters and tried to smile more, but many who had covered Bonds for years refused to trust it, and, in fact, they might be right that Bonds clearly does not enjoy performing the role of a happy, positive role model, as many fans expect a successful athlete should. When the public scorns successful athletes because they do not perform the role of the morally virtuous hero, however, it is not necessarily because the athlete is a bad person. It is more because sports stars like Bonds reveal the contradictions embodied in sports culture. As sports sociologist Matthew Goodman points out, sports are not necessarily the best arena in which to develop or display moral character.

> The very qualities a society tends to seek in its heroes—selflessness, social consciousness, and the like—are precisely the opposite of those needed to transform a talented but otherwise unremarkable neighborhood kid into a Michael Jordan or a Joe Montana. Becoming a star athlete requires a profound and long-term self-absorption, a single-minded attention to the development of a few rather odd physical skills, and an overarching competitive outlook. These qualities may well make a great athlete, but they don't necessarily make a great person.[5]

In fact, as Eitzen discussed, research supports Goodman's point. A study by sports sociologists Sharon Stoll and Jennifer Beller reveals that athletes score lower on moral development questionnaires than nonathletes.[6] By failing to cultivate a positive image, Bonds effectively exposes this contradiction. For example, Bonds will snap at reporters who attempt to interview him before games because it upsets his concentration, something that is central to his ability to focus properly. Bonds refuses to mentor his teammates in ways that might help them become better hitters because, in the contemporary free agent market, he is afraid they might end up playing against him and using the skills that he taught to defeat the Giants. Most recently, Bonds has withdrawn from his union's licensing agreement program—something that represents a break from solidarity with the very union that allowed him and his father to become wealthy—because he wants to maintain legal control over the public use of his image.[7]

None of these actions are things that one would consider acts of advanced moral character, yet all of them help him win, either on the field or in the marketplace of endorsement contracts. Bonds may indeed be selfish and rude, but if the sociological research is correct, then in fact this is what we should expect from most high-performing athletes in professional sports. At his core, Bonds might not be that different from the average professional athlete—neither any more self-absorbed nor any more arrogant nor any more rude. What has made him different is that he has never tried to project the image that he is better and that his overwhelming success makes it impossible for anyone to ignore him. It would be much easier if Barry Bonds were a failure, but he wins, and because of this, it is hard to reconcile his athletic success with his refusal to play the part of a virtuous sports hero.

The books and articles cited in the bibliography provide a useful range of perspectives on how sportswriters have viewed, reacted to, and interpreted Barry Bonds and to how Bonds has understood himself. In William Ladson's 1999 interview for the *Sporting News*, titled "The Complete Player," Bonds opens up and reflects upon his career and those who have been most important to him as a baseball player. Steve Travers, in his 2002 biography of Bonds, *Barry Bonds: Baseball's Superman*, and J. Pearlman in "Appreciating Bonds," his 2000 profile written for *Sports Illustrated*, present Bonds as a tempestuous, difficult, overpaid baseball star. Travers' work is one of the few book-length biographies of Bonds written for an adult audience. It is a particularly gossipy account, featuring discussions of spring training peccadilloes by several well-known players, little of which has to do with Bonds himself. What is more interesting is Travers' own attempt to reconcile aspects of Bonds' personality with Bonds' success as a player. Pearlman's article came after an eight-year vow of silence during which Bonds refused to talk to *Sports Illustrated*. Pearlman addresses the same dilemma as Travers, but concludes that the slugger is a changed man.

Josh Suchon's book, *This Gracious Season*, is an insider's account of Bonds' 2001 march toward seventy-three home runs. Suchon is a sportswriter for the *Oakland Tribune* who covered Bonds during that year. Reflecting the daily grind of a beat writer, Suchon presents Bonds in a uniquely demythologized fashion. His account follows the season chronologically, but along the way, he teaches readers a great deal about the lives and personalities of professional athletes and the media circus that surrounds them. In Suchon's book, Bonds is viewed as much like most Major League Baseball players, except for the fact that he is supremely talented. Unlike Suchon's book, David Grann's article for *The New York Times Magazine*, titled "Baseball without Metaphor," offers an account of Bonds during the 2002 season from the perspective of an outsider. Posing as a relatively naive interloper to the world of American sports journalism, Grann offers a fresh perspective on Bonds. His article addresses Bonds' personality, but it is more about the metaphors that baseball fans attach to their sport and the unrealistic expectations that these metaphors place upon how we imagine those who play the game.

Tim Keown, writing for *ESPN: The Magazine*, made an insightful observation about Barry Bonds during the season in which he hit seventy-three home runs. He quoted Bonds during an interview after a game as having explained his success at the plate in the following manner: "It's called talent. . . . I just have it. I can't explain it. You either have it or you don't, and I do. People always think there's an answer to everything, but there isn't. . . . When people see something they've never seen before, the first thing they say is, 'How did you do that?' The next thing is, 'Can you teach me?' The answer is no, because you don't have it." As Keown points out, most fans would probably agree with Bonds, yet he is not supposed to talk about himself in this manner. Sports fans expect their heroes to be humble and to play this role in public (no matter how self-centered they are in private). Bonds, however, refuses to play along and thus forces fans to think about their own expectations and ideas about athletes.[8]

> You come to Bonds holding a mirror. You want to hold that mirror up to him in such a way that everybody can see what you see. Difficult, tortured, perceptive, supremely talented—all of it. But you find that Bonds is holding his own mirror, forcing us to watch ourselves watch him. He turns his answers into questions, dispensing the discomfort where he sees fit. He wants to know: What do you see when you see him?[9]

Whether or not Barry Bonds is able to change his image is something that we can find out only by waiting. Many other athletes, including Bonds' father, his cousin Reggie Jackson, and his godfather, Willie Mays, had much more controversial images when they were players than they did after retirement. It is also uncertain whether Bonds will ever be able to overcome his own deep-seated distrust of the media, a distrust that goes back to the unfair treatment that he believes his father received. What is certain, however, is that fans actually know little about the players they admire. All they have to go on are the reports that they read in the papers and that they see on television. By investigating the personal popularity of players like Barry Bonds and by asking questions about the images associated with them, fans can at least learn a great deal about their own culture, its assumptions, and its prejudices, all of which are centrally important to the ways in which sports heroes are more than just players on a field; they are meaningful cultural icons.

NOTES

1. John Shea, "Bonds' HR One-Ups Mays: Slugger Stands Alone at No. 3," *San Francisco Chronicle*, April 14, 2004, D1.

2. John Rawlings and Ron Smith, "Better Player: Barry Bonds or Willie Mays?" *Sporting News*, September 22, 2003, 8.

3. Allen Wilson, "Bonds Still Not Touching All the Bases," *Buffalo News*, April 14, 2004.

4. Henry Yu, "Tiger Woods at the Center of History," in *Sports Matters: Race, Recreation, and Leisure*, eds. John Bloom and Michael Nevin Willard (New York: New York University Press, 2002), 320–353.

5. Matthew Goodman, "Where Have You Gone Joe DiMaggio," *Utne Reader* 57 (May/June 1993), 103; Goodman is also quoted in D. Stanley Eitzen, *Fair and Foul*, 55.

6. Eitzen, *Fair and Foul*, 53.

7. Ken Rosenthal, "Business as Usual for Bonds—He Comes First," *Sporting News*, December 1, 2003, 2.

8. Tim Keown, "Barry Feels Determined to Bring the Giants a Championship . . . and That's All," *ESPN: The Magazine*/ESPNMag.com, September 17, 2001, http://espn mag.com.

9. Ibid.

APPENDIX: BARRY BONDS' AWARDS AND CAREER AND POSTSEASON STATISTICS

College (Arizona State University):

Year	G	BA	AB	R	H	2B	3B	HR	RBI	SB/A	BB	SO
1983	64	.306	206	60	63	12	2	11	54	16/22	41	42
1984	70	.360	258	62	93	20	2	11	55	30/45	46	49
1985	62	.368	247	61	91	10	3	23	66	11/16	35	37

Minor League:

Year	Tm	Lg	Ag	Org	BA	G	AB	R	H	2B	3B	HR	RBI	SB	BB	SO	SLG
1985	Prince William	Caro.	21	PIT	.299	71	254	49	76	16	4	13	37	15	37	52	.547
1986	Hawaii	PCL	21	PIT	.311	44	148	30	46	7	2	7	37	16	33	31	.527

Major League:

Year	Ag	Tm	Lg	G	AB	R	H	2B	3B	HR	RBI	SB	CS	BB	SO	BA	OBP	SLG
1986	21	PIT	NL	113	413	72	92	26	3	16	48	36	7	65	102	.223	.330	.416
1987	22	PIT	NL	150	551	99	144	34	9	25	59	32	10	54	88	.261	.329	.492
1988	23	PIT	NL	144	538	97	152	30	5	24	58	17	11	72	82	.283	.368	.491
1989	24	PIT	NL	159	580	96	144	34	6	19	58	32	10	93	93	.248	.351	.426
1990	25	PIT	NL	151	519	104	156	32	3	33	114	52	13	93	83	.301	.406	.565
1991	26	PIT	NL	153	510	95	149	28	5	25	116	43	13	107	73	.292	.410	.514
1992	27	PIT	NL	140	473	109	147	36	5	34	103	39	8	127	69	.311	.456	.624
1993	28	SFG	NL	159	539	129	181	38	4	46	123	29	12	126	79	.336	.458	.677
1994	29	SFG	NL	112	391	89	122	18	1	37	81	29	9	74	43	.312	.426	.647

Year	Ag	Tm	Lg	G	AB	R	H	2B	3B	HR	RBI	SB	CS	BB	SO	BA	OBP	SLG
1995	30	SFG	NL	144	506	109	149	30	7	33	104	31	10	120	83	.294	.431	.577
1996	31	SFG	NL	158	517	122	159	27	3	42	129	40	7	151	76	.308	.461	.615
1997	32	SFG	NL	159	532	123	155	26	5	40	101	37	8	145	87	.291	.446	.585
1998	33	SFG	NL	156	552	120	167	44	7	37	122	28	12	130	92	.303	.438	.609
1999	34	SFG	NL	102	355	91	93	20	2	34	83	15	2	73	62	.262	.389	.617
2000	35	SFG	NL	143	480	129	147	28	4	49	106	11	3	117	77	.306	.440	.688
2001	36	SFG	NL	153	476	129	156	32	2	73	137	13	3	177	93	.328	.515	.863
2002	37	SFG	NL	143	403	117	149	31	2	46	110	9	2	198	47	.370	.582	.799
2003	38	SFG	NL	130	390	111	133	22	1	45	90	7	0	148	58	.341	.529	.749
Totals				2569	8725	1941	2595	536	74	658	1742	500	140	2070	1387	.297	.433	.602

POSTSEASON BATTING STATISTICS:

Year	Round	Tm	Opp	WL	G	AB	R	H	2B	3B	HR	RBI	BB	SO	BA	OBP	SLG	SB
1990	NLCS	PIT	CIN	L	6	18	4	3	0	0	0	1	6	6	.167	.375	.167	2
1991	NLCS	PIT	ATL	L	7	27	1	4	1	0	0	0	2	4	.148	.207	.185	3
1992	NLCS	PIT	ATL	L	7	23	5	6	1	0	1	2	6	4	.261	.414	.435	1
1997	NLDS1	SFG	FLA	L	3	12	0	3	2	0	0	2	0	3	.250	.250	.417	1
2000	NLDS2	SFG	NYM	L	4	17	2	3	1	1	0	1	3	4	.176	.300	.353	1
2002	NLDS1	SFG	ATL	W	5	17	2	3	1	1	0	1	3	4	.176	.300	.353	0
2002	NLCS	SFG	STL	W	5	11	5	3	0	1	1	1	10	2	.273	.619	.727	0
	WS	SFG	ANA	L	7	17	8	8	2	0	4	6	13	3	.471	.700	1.294	0
2003	NLDS2	SFG	FLA	L	4	9	3	2	1	0	0	2	8	0	.222	.556	.333	1
Totals				2-7	48	151	33	37	8	2	9	24	52	26	.245	.433	.503	9

1990, 1992, 1993, 1994, 1995, 1996, 1997, 2000, 2001, 2002, 2003.

LED THE LEAGUE IN THE FOLLOWING CATEGORIES BY YEAR:

Batting Ave.	Runs	RBI	Home Runs	On Base Pct.	Slugging Pct.
2002–370	1992–109	1993–123	1993–46	1991–410	1990–565
			2001–73	1992–456	1992–624
			(ML Record)		
				1993–458	1993–677
				1995–431	2001–863
					(ML Record)
				2001–515	2002–799
				2002–582	2003–749
				(ML Record)	
				2003–529	

AWARDS:

1990: NL Gold Glove (outfield)
1990: NL Most Valuable Player
1991: NL Gold Glove
1992: NL Gold Glove
1992: NL Most Valuable Player
1993: NL Gold Glove
1993: NL Most Valuable Player
1994: NL Gold Glove
1996: NL Gold Glove
1997: NL Gold Glove
1998: NL Gold Glove
2001: NL Most Valuable Player
2002: NL Most Valuable Player
2003: NL Most Valuable Player

A = assists; AB = at-bats; BA = batting average; E = errors; FA = fielding average; G = games; H = hits; HR = home runs; PO = put-outs; R = runs; RBI = runs batted in; 2B = doubles; 3B = triples

Sources

College Statistics: Arizona State University Official Athletic Site: Baseball: http://thesundevils.ocsn.com/sports/m-basebl/spec-rel/bonds-watch.html.

Minor League Statistics: Baseball Cube Stats Web Site: Barry Bonds: http://www.sports-wired.com/players/profile.asp?NameAJE.

Major League Statistics: Baseball-Reference.com: Barry Bonds Statistics: http://www.baseball-reference.com/b/bondsba01.shtml.

SELECTED BIBLIOGRAPHY

BIOGRAPHIES OF BARRY BONDS

Suchon, Josh. *This Gracious Season: Barry Bonds and the Greatest Year in Baseball*. Winter Publications, 2002.

Travers, Steve. *Barry Bonds: Baseball's Superman*. Champaign, IL: Sports Publishing, LLC, 2002.

MAGAZINE PROFILES OF BARRY BONDS

Grann, David. "Baseball without Metaphor." *The New York Times Magazine*, September 1, 2002.

Ladson, William. "The Complete Player." *Sporting News*, June 12, 1999, 12.

Pearlman, J. "Appreciating Bonds: Though Obscured by the Home Run Barrage, an Older, Wiser Barry Bonds Is in Many Ways Better Than Ever." *Sports Illustrated*, June 5, 2000, 48–50, 53.

BOOKS, ARTICLES, AND MONOGRAPHS ON BASEBALL

Feinstein, John. *Play Ball: The Life and Troubled Times of Major League Baseball*. New York: Villard Books, 1993.

Marini, Matthew. *Home Run Heroes: Press Coverage for Roger Maris, Mark McGwire, and Barry Bonds*. M.A. thesis, California State University Northridge.

Staudohar, Paul D. "The Baseball Strike of 1994–95." *Monthly Labor Review* 120, no. 3 (March 1997): 21–28.

BOOKS ON HISTORY AND SOCIOLOGY OF SPORTS

Bloom, John, and Michael Nevin Willard, eds. *Sports Matters: Race, Recreation, and Culture.* New York: New York University Press, 2002.
Eitzen, D. Stanley. *Fair and Foul: Beyond the Myths and Paradoxes of Sport.* Lanham, MD: Rowman and Littlefield, 2003.
Riley, James A. *The Biographical Encyclopedia of Negro Baseball Leagues.* New York: Carroll and Graf, 1994.
Ruck, Rob. *Sandlot Seasons: Sport in Black Pittsburgh.* Urbana: University of Illinois Press, 1987.
Wiggins, David K., and Patrick B. Miller. *The Unlevel Playing Field: A Documentary History of the African American Experience in Sport.* Urbana: University of Illinois Press, 2003.

JUVENILE LITERATURE BIOGRAPHIES OF BARRY BONDS

Bernstein, Ross. *Barry Bonds.* Minneapolis: Lerner Sports, 2004.
Dougherty, Terri. *Barry Bonds.* Edina, MN: Abdo Publications, 2002.
Harvey, Miles. *Barry Bonds: Baseball's Complete Player.* Chicago: Children's Press, 1994.
Miller, Raymond. *Barry Bonds.* San Diego: Kid Haven Press, 2003.
Muskat, Carrie. *Barry Bonds.* Philadelphia: Chelsea House, 1997.
Savage, Jeff. *Barry Bonds: Mr. Excitement.* Minneapolis: Lerner Publications, 1997.
Thornley, Stew. *Super Sports Star Barry Bonds.* Berkeley Heights, NJ: Enslow, 2004.

WEB SITES

Allen Barra. Salon.com. Discusses Bonds record-breaking home-run year in 2001. http://www.salon.com/news/sports/col/barra/2002/03/28/bonds/.
Arizona State University Sun Devils. Contains statistics and information about Bonds' college career. http://thesundevils.ocsn.com/sports/m-basebl/spec-rel/bonds-watch.html.
Barry Bonds' official Web site. http://www.barrybonds.com.
ESPN. Contains David Halberstam's columns and Ralph Wiley's column on Barry Bonds. http://espn.go.com/page2.html.
Everwonder. An unofficial fan Web site providing a biographical sketch of Bonds. http://www.everwonder.com/david/bonds/info.htm.

Selected Bibliography

Junior Baseball magazine. An interview with Bonds with childhood photos of the slugger. Bonds discusses his own childhood and his memories of playing baseball
  in high school. http://wwwjuniorbaseball.com/wheniwasakid/bonds.shtml.
PSA, Professional Sports Authenticator. A baseball card collectors' Web site with a good,
  short biography of Bonds. http://www.psacard.com/articles/article3223.chtml.
San Francisco Giants. Follow the links from the button marked "The Giants" to find
  vital statistics and biographical information on Bonds and other players.
  http://sanfrancisco.giants.mlb.com.

INDEX

Aaron, Hank, 91

Adams, Terry, 68

African Americans, athletes, 3; in baseball, 94; criticism directed toward in sports, 52

Alger, Hortio, 116

Alou, Felipe, 89; hired as manager of San Francisco Giants, 87

Alou Brothers (Felipe, Jose, Matty), 4, 5

Anaheim Angels, 84

Anderson, Garret, 85

Anderson, Greg, 97, 99, 104

Anderson, Sparky, 24

Angell, Roger, 71

Arizona State University, 10; placed on NCAA probation, 11

Arnold, Tom, 108

Aschburner, Steve, 37

Ashcroft, John, 101

Atherton, California, 40

Atlanta Braves, 25

Aurilia, Rich, 74

Avery, Steve, 25, 26

Babe Ruth Birthplace Museum, 92

Backman, Wally, 22

Baker, Dusty, xx, 32, 57, 72, 79; connection to Bonds family in Riverside, California, 33; leaves Giants to manage Chicago Cubs, 87

Barra, Allan, 83–84, 93

Bay Area Laboratory Cooperative (BALCO), 97, 99–111

Belinda, Stan, 27

Bell, Gus and Buddy, 19

Beller, Jennifer, 118

Benard, Marvin, 107

Benzinger, Todd, 72

Berryhill, Damon, 27

Bertetta, Russ, 9

The Birth of a Nation, 41

Blackstone, John, 73

Bock, Hal, 42

Bodley, Hal, 69

Bogle, Donald, 53

Bonds, Aisha Lynn, 61

Bonds, Barry: birth, 4; contract, 67; death threats, 73; divorce, 40–43; drafted by Pittsburgh Pirates, 12; early distrust of media, 7; legal case over possession of single-season record home-run ball, 77; marriage to Sun Bonds, 42; negative public image, xviii–xix; not liking to be called "Bobby," 18; passes Willie Mays on all-time home-run career home-run list, 115; race as a factor in his public image, xix; record breaking home runs until 2001, xvii, 74; selected to All Star Game for the first time, 20; signs first contract with the San Francisco Giants, 31; wins first Most Valuable Player Award (MVP), 21; wins sixth MVP, 96

Bonds, Bobby, 5–6, 21, 91; biography, 1, 3–4; death during 2003 season, 95

Bonds, Liz, 89

Bonds, Nikolai, 61

Bonds, Patricia, 4

Bonds, Rosie, 4

Bonds, Shikari, 61

Bonds, Sun, 26; divorce from Barry, 40–42

Bonilla, Bobby, 21, 22, 25, 60

Boone, Bob, 17

Boras, Scott, 67–68, 78

Boswell, Thomas, 27, 33, 36, 95

Brady, Tom, 8

Bream, Sid, xix, 12, 18, 22, 26, 27

Brock, Barry, 35

Brock, Jim, 10, 11

Brown, Willie, 55

Burlingame, California, 95

Bush, President George W., 100, 101

Cabrera, Francisco, 27

Caminiti, Ken, 82

Candiotti, Tom, 43

Candlestick Park (later 3-Com Park), 50, 53–55

Canziani, Dave, 9

Cardenal, José, 5

CBS, 46, 73

Cepeda, Orlando, 5

Cerrone, Rick, 35

Chicago Cubs, 87, 96

Clark, Will, 32

Clayton, Royce, 33

Clinton, President Bill, 74

CNN, 74

Cohn, Lowell, 36

College World Series, 10, 11

Colletti, 95

Collier, Gene, 25

Conte, Victor Jr., 97, 102, 104, 106

Corbett, Jim, 41

Cowlings, Al, 41

Dierker, Larry, 73

Dominican Republic, 4

Donahue, Kevin, 9

Drabek, Doug, 18, 20, 21, 22, 25, 26

Dunston, Shawn, 74

Dykstra, Lenny, 43

Eitzen, D. Stanley, 56, 116

Elias Sports Bureau, 20

Enron, 100

Enron Field, 73

Erstad, Darin, 85

ESPN, 82

ESPN.com, 69

ESPN: The Magazine, 119

Estes, Shawn, 63, 68

Fainaru-Wada, Mark, 107

Feinstein, John, 34

Figueroa, Ed, 5

Fimrite, Ron, 95

Fischel, John, 43

Flood, Curt, 45

Florida Marlins, 96

Foster, George, 5

Fox News Channel, 108

Fregosi, Jim, 7

Gagne, Eric, 91

Gant, Ron, 26, 27

Giambi, Jason, 102, 103, 107

Gibbons, Michael, 92

Gibson, Josh, 92
Gilbert, Dennis, 35
Gilded Age, 57
Glaus, Troy, 85
Glavine, Tom, 25, 26
Goldman, Ronald, 40
Gonzalez, Luis, 66
Gooden, Dwight, 12
Goodman, Matthew, 118
Grace, Mark, 65
Grann, David, 4, 5, 84, 119
Greenfield, Jeff, 101
Gretsky, Wayne, 110
Griffey, Ken Jr., 65
Guerrero, Vladimir, 91
Gwynn, Tony, 39

Haak, Howie, 12
Halberstam, 69, 70–71, 72, 86–87
Hall, Stuart, 52
Harrisburg (Pennsylvania) Patriot News, 99
Hayashi, Patrick, 77
Hayward, California 95
Hertzel, Bob, 23
Hoffer, Richard, 35–36
HOK Sports, 55
Holley, Robert, 106
Honeycutt, Rick, 13
Houston Astros, 77
Hunter, Brian, 27

Institute for Diversity and Ethics in Sport, 94
integration of professional sports, 4
Internal Revenue Service, 107, 109
Irvin, Monte, 4

Jackson, Reggie, xx, 5, 10
Jefferies, Gregg, 8
Jenkins, Bruce, 33
Johnson, Ben, 53
Johnson, Charles, 66
Johnson, Jack, 41
Johnson, Randy, 96

Jones, Marion, 97
Jordan, Michael, 36, 69, 117
Junipero Serra High School, 7, 8

Kent, Jeff, 53, 58, 68, 72, 75, 79, 80, 81, 89; conflicts with Bonds, 58–59; wins MVP in 2000, 67
Keown, Tim, 31, 50, 59, 119
King, Jeff, 36
Kinney, Matt, 110
Kirkland, Willie, 5
Korchenmny, Remi, 104
Kozloski, Judge Judith, 42
Krukow, Mike, 51
Ku Klux Klan, 41
Kurkjian, Tim, 27

Lachimia, Jim, 23
Ladson, William, 118
Lapchick, Richard, 94
LaValliere, Mike, 27, 28
Leyland, Jim, 13, 18, 20, 22, 28, 34, 51, 53, 60, 67; public argument with Bonds at training camp, 23–24
Limbaugh, Rush, 46
Lipsitz, George, 56
Lofton, Kenny, 84
Los Angeles Dodgers, 66
Lurie, Bob, 32

Maddux, Greg, 34
Magowan, Peter, 32, 55, 56, 68, 78, 99
Major League Players Association, 39
Maldinaldo, Candy, 43
Maris, Roger, 58, 105
Mays, Willie, xix, 4, 5, 65, 68, 91, 102
McCovey, Willie, 5, 68
McCovey Cove, 56, 66
McDowell, Jack, 10
McGraw, John, 44
McGriff, Fred, 34
McGwire, Mark, 65, 66, 69, 87
McKeon, Jack, 96
McKercher, Bob, 7, 9

McMurtry, Craig, 13
Meersand, Alan, 43
Meyer, Paul, 60
Michigan Militia, 49
Miller, Marvin, 45
Miller, Patrick, 1
Miller, Stu, 54
Montgomery, Tim, 97
Mota, Manny, 5
Mueller, 60
Muscle and Fitness Online, 104
"Muscular Christianity," 116

National Public Radio (NPR), 69
Neagle, Denny, 103
Negro Leagues Baseball Museum, 91
Nen, Rob, 67
Nevius, C. W., 52
New York Yankees, 5, 96
Newhan, Ross, 80, 92
Nixon, Richard, 54
Novitsky, Jeff, 107, 109

Oakland Tribune, 68
Olson, Drew, 92
O'Neil, Buck, 92
Orange County, California, 58
O'Reilly, Bill, 108
Oriole Park at Camden Yards, 55
Oswalt, Roy, 109

Pac Bell Park, 56, 57, 66
Packard Stadium, 11
Pagan, José, 5
Paige, Woody, 23, 24
Park, Chan Ho, xvii, 73–74
Payne, Anna, 71
Peace, Jennifer, 41
Pearlman, 63, 119
Pendleton, Terry, 25, 27
Pittsburgh Pirates, 17–28
Pittsburgh Post-Gazette, 23

Playboy, 109
Popov, Alex, 77
Power, Ted, 22
Prince William (class A baseball team), 12
Puckett, Kirby, 117

Quest Diagnostics, 110

Rains, Michael, 107
Ramirez, Manny, 67
Ratto, Ray, 81, 100
Rawlings, John, 115–116
Reilly, Rick, 69, 77, 72, 85–86
reserve clause, 6; struck down by United States Supreme Court, 45
Reynolds, R. J., 22
Ripkin, Cal Jr., 74
Riverside, California, 3–4
Rodriguez, Alex, 67, 91
Romanowski, 107
Rose, Pete, 21
Rosenthal, Ken, 74, 95
Russell, Bill, 110
Ruth, Babe, 71, 91

Sabean, Brian, 58, 59, 67
Safeway (supermarket chain), 32
Salmon, Tim, 85
San Carlos, California, 5
San Francisco Giants, build new stadium, 55; loss of attendance after baseball strike, 50; sign Bonds as a free agent, 28
San Mateo, California, 7
San Mateo County, California, 40
Santa Clara County, California, 55
Santiago, Benito, 91, 100, 107
Selig, Bud, 106
September 11, 2001, 73
Serra, J. Tony, 106
Seymour, Gene, 41

Sheffield, Gary, 106, 107
Siegel, Robert, 69
Simmons, Lon, 54
Simpson, Nicole Browne, 40
Simpson, O. J., 40, 41, 72
Smalley, Roy Jr., 17
Smith, Claire, 24
Smith, Ron, 115–116
Smizik, Bob, 28
Smoltz, John, 25, 26
Snow, J. T., 68
Sotomayer, Sonia, 49
Sporting News, 19; awards Bonds "Player of the Decade," 63
Sports Illustrated, 27, 63, 69, 72, 94, 105, 117
Stanford University, 12
State of the Union Address, 100
Staudohar, Paul, 45
Steele, David, 18, 57, 87
steroids, 82–84; results of league testing in 2003, 106
Stoll, Sharon, 118
Stoneham, Horace, 4, 54
Suchon, Josh, 7, 32, 51, 58, 65, 68, 70, 78, 119
Swan, Lynn, 7
Sweeney, John, 107

Tanner, Chuck, 12
Tartabul, José, 5
Taylor, George, 41
THG (steroid), 102, 110
Thomas, Frank, 37
Three Rivers Stadium, 25
Thrift, Syd, 13, 18
Travers, Steve, 119
Treder, Steve, 5

U.S. Justice Department, 101
U.S. Olympic Committee, 101
U.S. Olympic Team, 4
U.S. Supreme Court, 6
USA Today, 31, 69
University of Southern California, 10

Valente, James J., 102
Van Dyken, Amy, 97
Van Slyke, 12, 18, 21, 22, 25
Velarde, Randy, 107
Verducci, Tom, 94, 106
Vincent, Faye, 46
Virden, Bill, 23
Vogel, Randy, 8

Wakefield, Tim, 26
Walk, Bob, 26
Ward, John Montgomery, 44
Watson, Liz, 61
Wells, Kip, 82
Wendell, Turk, 103, 104
White, Devon, 60
Wiggins, David, 1
Wilbon, Michael, 39
Wiley, Ralph, 93–94
Williams, Lance, 107
Williams, Matt, 32, 39, 58, 67
Williams, Ted, 79
Wilson, Allen, 116
Woods, Tiger, 69, 117
World Series, cancellation in 1994, 39, 44; 2002 series, 84–87
World War II, 4
Worrell, 85

Yu, Henry, 116–117

About the Author

JOHN BLOOM teaches American Studies at the University of Maryland at Baltimore County. He is the author of several articles and books about sports and culture in the United States, including *A House of Cards: Baseball Card Collecting and Popular Culture* and *To Show What an Indian Can Do: Sports at Indian Boarding Schools*, both published by the University of Minnesota Press. He is also the co-editor, along with Michael Nevin Willard, of *Sports Matters: Race, Recreation, and Culture*, published by New York University Press. He lives in Carlisle, Pennsylvania, with his wife, Amy Farrell, his children, Catherine and Nicholas, and his two cats, Larry and Darrell.